B. L. Abrahams

The Expulsion of the Jews from England in 1290

B. L. Abrahams

The Expulsion of the Jews from England in 1290

ISBN/EAN: 9783337132965

Printed in Europe, USA, Canada, Australia, Japan

Cover: Foto ©ninafisch / pixelio.de

More available books at **www.hansebooks.com**

Arnold Prize Essay, 1894.

THE EXPULSION OF THE JEWS FROM ENGLAND IN 1290

BY

B. L. ABRAHAMS

Formerly Scholar of Balliol College.

Oxford

B. H. BLACKWELL 50 and 51, BROAD STREET

London

SIMPKIN, MARSHALL, HAMILTON, KENT & CO.

———

M DCCC XCV

This Essay, to which the Arnold Prize in the University of Oxford was awarded in 1894, has appeared in the *Jewish Quarterly Review* for October, 1894, and January and April, 1895. I am indebted to the Editors of the *Review* for permission to republish it.

I wish to express my obligations to *Bibliotheca Anglo-Judaica : a Bibliographical Guide to Anglo-Jewish History*, compiled by Messrs. JOSEPH JACOBS and LUCIEN WOLF, and to *The Jews of Angevin England*, by Mr. JOSEPH JACOBS. Nearly all the passages bearing on Anglo-Jewish history, down to 1206, are contained in the latter book, and many of the references in the earlier part of my essay might have been made to its pages. I thought it better, however, to refer direct to the original authorities, and have, as a rule, mentioned Mr. Jacobs' book only when using passages in it which have been nowhere else printed.

Some articles which I have contributed to Mr. R. H. I. PALGRAVE'S *Dictionary of Political Economy*, to the First Volume of the *Transactions of the Jewish Historical Society of England*, and to the *Jewish Chronicle* for April 26th, 1895, contain information bearing on the subject of this Essay.

THE EXPULSION OF THE JEWS FROM ENGLAND IN 1290.

THE expulsion of the Jews from England by Edward I. is a measure concerning the causes of which no contemporary historian gives, or pretends to give, any but the most meagre information. It was passed by the King in his " secret council," of the proceedings of which we naturally know nothing. Of the occasion that suggested it, each separate writer has his own account, and none has a claim to higher authority than the rest; and yet there is much in the circumstances connected with it that calls for explanation. How was it that, at a time when trade and the need for capital were growing, the Jews, who were reputed to be among the great capitalists of Europe, were expelled from England ? How did Edward, a king who was in debt from the moment he began his reign till the end, bring himself to give up the revenue that his father and grandfather had derived from the Jews ? How could he, as an honourable king, drive out subjects who were protected by a Charter that one of his predecessors had granted, and another had solemnly confirmed ? To answer these questions we must consider what was the position that the Jews occupied in England, how it was forced on them, and how it brought them into antagonism at various times with the interests of the several orders of the English people, and with the teachings of the Catholic Church. We shall thus find the origin of forces strong enough when they converged to bring about the result which is to be accounted for.

I.—THE JEWS FROM THEIR ARRIVAL TO 1190.

Among the foreigners who flocked to England at, or
soon after, the Conquest were many families of French
Jews. They brought with them money, but no skill in
any occupation except that of lending it out at interest.
They lent to the King, when the ferm of his counties, or his
feudal dues were late in coming in ;[1] to the barons, who,
though lands and estates had been showered on them,
nevertheless often found it hard, without doubt, to procure
ready money wherewith to pay for luxuries, or to meet
the expense of military service ; and to suitors who had to
follow the King's Court from one great town to another,
or to plead before the Papal Curia at Rome.[2]

But though they thus came into contact with many
classes, and had kindly relations with some, they remained
far more alien to the masses of the people around them
than even the Normans, in whose train they had come to
England. Even the Norman baron must, a hundred years
after the Conquest, have become something of an Englishman. He held an estate, of which the tenants were English ;
he presided over a court attended by English suitors. In
battle he led his English retainers. He and the Englishman worshipped in the same church, and in it the sons of
the two might serve as priests side by side. But the Jews
remained, during the whole time of their sojourn in England, sharply separated from, at any rate, the common
people around them by peculiarities of speech, habits and
daily life, such as must have aroused dread ·and hatred in
an ignorant and superstitious age. Their foreign faces
alone would have been enough to mark them out.
Moreover, they generally occupied, not under compulsion,
but of their own choice, a separate quarter of each town

---

[1] J. Jacobs, *Jews of Angevin England,* 43-4 ; 64-5.

[2] Cf. the account of the litigation of Richard of Anesty in Palgrave's
Rise and Progress of the English Commonwealth, Vol. II. (Proofs and
Illustrations), pp. xxiv.-xxvii.

in which they dwelt.[1] And in their isolation they
lived a life unlike that of any other class. None of
them were feudal landowners, none farmers, none villeins,
none members of the guilds. They did not join in
the national Watch and Ward. They alone were forbidden to keep the mail and hauberk which the rest
of the nation was bound to have at hand to help in pre-
serving the peace.[2] They were not enrolled in the Frank-
pledge, that society that brought neighbours together and
taught them to be interested in the doings of one another
by making them responsible for one another's honesty.
They did not appear at the Court Leet or the Court Baron,
at the Town-moot or the Shire-moot. They went to no
church on Sundays, they took no sacrament ; they showed
no signs of reverence to the crucifix ; but, instead, they
went on Friday evening and Saturday morning to a syna-
gogue of their own, where they read a service in a foreign
tongue, or sang it to strange Oriental melodies. When
they died they were buried in special cemeteries, where
Jews alone were laid.[3] At home their very food was
different from that of Christians. They would not eat
of a meal prepared by a Christian cook in a Christian
house. They would not use the same milk, the same wine,
the same meat as their neighbours. For them cattle had
to be killed with special rites ; and, what was worse, it
sometimes happened that, some minute detail having been
imperfectly performed, they rejected meat as unfit for
themselves, but considered it good enough to be offered
for sale to their Christian neighbours.[1] The presence of

---

[1] See Jewries of Oxford and Winchester, in the plans in Norgate's
England under Angevin Kings. I., pp. 31, 40 ; and Jewry of London, described in *Papers of Anglo-Jewish Historical Exhibition*, pp. 20-52.
[2] *Chronica Rogeri de Hoveden* (Rolls Series) II., 261 ; *Gesta Henrici
II. et Ricardi I.* (Rolls Series), I. 279.
[3] *Gesta Henrici II. et Ricardi I.* (R. S.), I. 182 ; *Chronica Rogeri de
Hoveden* (R. S.). II. 137.
[4] Depping, *Les Juifs dans le Moyen Age*, 170 ; Jacobs' *The Jews of
Angevin England.* 54, 178 ; *Statutes of the Realm* (Edition of 1810), I. 202

Christian servants and nurses in their households made it impossible that any of their peculiarities should remain unobserved or generally unknown.[1]

Thus, living as semi-aliens, growing rich as usurers, and observing strange customs, they occupied in the twelfth century a position that was fraught with danger. But, almost from their first arrival in the country, they had enjoyed a kind of informal Royal protection,[2] though, as to the nature of their relations with the King during the first hundred and thirty years of their residence, very little is known. It was probably less close than it afterwards became, for the liability to attack and the need for protection had not yet manifested themselves.

But, at the end of the eleventh century, there began to spread throughout Europe a movement which, when it reached England, converted the vague popular dislike of the Jews into an active and violent hostility. While the Norman conquerors were still occupied in settling down in England, the King organising his realm, and the barons enjoying, dissipating, or forfeiting their newly-won estates, popes and priests and monks had been preaching the Crusade to the other nations of civilised Europe. At one of the greatest and most imposing of all the Church Councils that were ever held, where were present lay nobles and clerics of all nations, attending each as his own master, and able to act on the impulse of the moment, Urban II., in 1095, told the tale of the wrong that

---

(Judicium Pillorie) and 203 (Statutum de Pistoribus). See also *Leet Jurisdiction in Norwich* (Selden Society, 1891), p. 28, where, in a list of amercements inflicted at the Leet of Nedham and Manecroft, the following entry occurs :—" De Johanne le Pastemakere quia vendidit Carnes quas Judei vocant trefa, 2s."

[1] Mansi, *Sacrorum Conciliorum Collectio*, Venice, 1775, XX.399 ; Wilkins, *Concilia Magnae Britanniae*, I. 591, 675, 719 ; *Gesta Henrici II. et Ricardi I.* (R. S.), I. 230. *Chronica Rogeri de Hoveden* (R. S.), II. 180.

[2] Cf. the words of John's Charter : " Libertates et consuetudines sicut eas habuerunt tempore Henrici avi patris nostri."—*Rotuli Chartarum*, p. 93.

Christians had to suffer at the hands of the enemies of Christ. He told his hearers how the Eastern people, a people estranged from God, had laid waste the land of the Christians with fire and sword ; had destroyed churches, or misused them for their own rites ; had circumcised Christians, poured their blood on altars and fonts, scourged and impaled men, and dishonoured women.[1] Such denunciations, followed by the appeal to all present to help Jerusalem, which was "ruled by enemies, enslaved by the godless, and calling aloud to be freed," excited, for the first time in Europe, a furious and fanatical hatred of Eastern and non-Christian races. The Jews were such a race, as well as the Saracens, and between the two the Crusaders scarcely distinguished. Before they left home and fortune to fight God's enemies abroad, it was natural that they should kill or convert those whom they met nearer home. Through all central Europe, from France to Hungary, the bands that gathered together to make their way to the Holy Land fell on the Jews and offered them the choice between the sword and the font.[2]

The disasters that followed the first Crusade brought with them an increase in the ferocity of the attacks to which the Jews of Continental Europe were subjected, and S. Bernard, when he preached the second Crusade, found that he had revived a spirit of fanaticism that he was powerless to quell. He had wished for the reconquest of the Holy Land as a result that would bring honour to the Christian religion ; but his followers and imitators thought less of the end than of the bloodshed that was

---

[1] *Recueil des Historiens des Croisades—Historiens Occidentaux* (Paris, 1866), III. 321, 727. Cf. especially (p. 727), Altaria suis foeditatibus inquinata subvertunt, Christianos circumcidunt, cruoremque circumcisionis aut super altaria fundunt aut in vasis baptisterii immergunt (Roberti Monachi *Historia Iherosolimitana*).

[2] Neubauer and Stern, *Hebräische Berichte über die Judenverfolgungen während der Kreuzzüge* ; Hefele, *Conciliengeschichte*, V., 224, 270 ; Graetz, *Geschichte der Juden* (second edition) VI., 89-107.

to be the means. A monk, "who skilfully imitated the
austerity of religion, but had no immoderate amount of
learning,"[1] went through the Rhineland preaching that all
Jews who were found by the Crusaders should be killed
as enemies of the Christian faith. It was in vain that
Bernard appealed to the Christian nations whom his elo-
quence had aroused, in the hope that "the zeal of God which
burnt in them would not fail altogether to be tempered
with knowledge." He himself narrowly escaped attack ;
and the Jews suffered from the second Crusade as they had
suffered from the first.[2]

England was so closely related to the Churches of the
Continent that it could not fail to be affected by the great
movement. But the first Crusade was preached when the
Conquest was still recent, and the Normans had no leisure
to leave their new country ; the second, during the last
period of anarchy in the reign of Stephen.

Thus there were, during the first hundred years after the
Council of Clermont, few English Crusaders. Yet the Crusading spirit, working in a superstitious mediaeval popula-
tion, called forth a danger that was destined to be as fatal
to the English Jews as were the massacres to their brethren
on the Continent. The Pope who preached the first Crusade had told his hearers that Eastern nations were in the
habit of circumcising Christians and using their blood in
such a way as to show their contempt for the Christian
religion. This charge was naturally extended to the Jews
as well. What alterations it underwent in its circulation it
is hard to say ; but in 1146, a tale was spread among the
populace of Norwich, and encouraged by the bishop, that
the Jews had killed a boy named William, to use his blood
for the ritual of that most suspicious feast, their Passover.
The story was supported by no evidence more trustworthy
than that of an apostate Jew, which was so worthless that

[1] C. U. Hahn, *Geschichte der Ketzer im Mittelalter*, III. 17.
[2] Graetz, *Geschichte der Juden* (second edition), VI., 155-170. Cf.
Hefele, V., 498, n 2.

the Sheriff refused to allow the Jews to appear in the
Bishop's Court to answer the charge brought against
them, and took them under his protection. But the
popular suspicion of the Jews lent credibility to the
story, and so terrible a feeling was aroused that many of
the Jews of Norwich dispersed into other lands, and of
those who remained many were killed by the people in
spite of the protection of the Sheriff.[1] The accusation once
made naturally recurred, first at Gloucester, in 1168, and
then at Bury St. Edmund's, in 1181. "The Martyrs" were
regularly buried in the nearest church or religious house,
and the miracles that they all worked would alone have
been enough to continually renew the belief in the terrible
story.[2]

Under the firm reign of Henry II., anti-Jewish feeling
found no further expression in act. The King, like his
predecessors, gave and secured to the Jews special privileges so great as to arouse the envy of their neighbours.
They were allowed to settle their own disputes in their
own *Beth Din*, or Ecclesiastical Court, and in so far to enjoy
a privilege that was granted only under strict limitations
to the Christian Church.[3] They were placed, apparently,
under the special protection of the royal officers of each
district.[4] They lived in safety, and they made considerable
contributions to the Royal Exchequer.

The death of Henry II. and the accession of Richard I.,
the first English Crusading King, brought trouble, as
was but natural, to the rich and royally favoured infidels

[1] Jacobs, *Op. Cit.*, 20, 257.

[2] *Historia et Cartularium Monasterii S. Petri Gloucestriae* (R. S.), I.,
21 ; *Chronica Jocelini de Brakelonda* (Camden Society), 12, 113-14 ;
Annales Monastici (R. S.), I., 343, II., 347 ; Matt. Paris, *Chronica
Majora* (R. S.), IV., 377, V., 518 ; Jacobs' *Jews of Angevin England*, 19 ;
and cf. *Chronicles of Reigns of Stephen, Henry II., Richard I.* (Rolls
Series), I., 311.

[3] *Materials for History of Thomas Becket* (Rolls Series), IV. 118 ;
Jacobs, *Jews of Angevin England*, 43, 155.

[4] Cf. the protection given to Jews of Norwich by the Sheriff (Jacobs,
257).

of the land where the blood accusation had its birth. The interregnum between the death of one King and the proclamation of the "peace" of his successor was always a time of danger and lawlessness during the first two centuries after the Conquest, and the growth of the crusading spirit, and of the popular belief in the truth of the blood accusation, caused all the forces of disorder to work in one direction, viz., against the Jews. The day of Richard's coronation was the first opportunity for a great exhibition of the anti-Jewish fanaticism of the populace. The nobles from all parts of the country brought with them to London large trains of servants and attendants, who were left to occupy themselves as best they might in the streets, while their lords were present at the ceremony. The Jews, who had been refused permission to enter the Abbey, took up a prominent position outside. Their appearance exasperated the crowd, and in the mediæval world a crowd was irresistible. While the service was proceeding, the Jews were fiercely attacked by the "wild serving men" of the nobles and the lower orders of citizens. One at least was compelled to accept baptism to save himself from death. Later in the same day, when the King and magnates were banqueting in the palace, the attack on the Jews was renewed. The strong houses of the Jewry were besieged and fired, and the inhabitants were massacred. But soon "avarice got the better of cruelty," and in spite of the efforts of the King's officers the city was given up to plunder and rapine.[1]

Though the King was bitterly angry at what had happened, the first attempt at punishment showed him how powerless he was against the forces hostile to the Jews. Had the offenders been nobles or prominent citizens, he could, when the first irresistible disorder had subsided, have taken vengeance at his leisure. But what could he do against a collection of serving-men and poor citizens, whom

---

[1] *Chronicles of the Reigns of Stephen, Henry II., and Richard I.* (Rolls Series), I. 294-9.

no one knew, who had come together and had separated in one day? When he departed for the Crusades, he left behind him all the materials for more outbreaks of the same kind. In the more populous towns Crusaders were continually gathering together in order to set out for the Holy Land in company: and they, aided by the lower citizens, clerics, and poor countrymen, and in some cases by ruined landholders, fell on and killed the Jews wherever they had settlements in England, at Norwich, York, Bury St. Edmunds, Lynn, Lincoln, Colchester, and Stamford.[1] Again the Royal officers were unable to touch the offenders. When the Chancellor arrived with an army at York, the scene of the most horrible of all the massacres, he found that the murderers were Crusaders, who had long embarked for the Holy Land, peasants and poor townsmen who had retired from the neighbourhood, and some bankrupt nobles, who had fled to Scotland. The citizens humbly represented that they were not responsible for the outrage and were too weak to prevent it. No punishment was possible except the infliction of a few fines, and the Chancellor marched back with his army to London.[2]

It was clear that the King must strengthen his connection with the Jews. He could not afford to lose them or to leave them continually liable to plunder. They were too rich. In 1187, when Henry II. had wanted to raise a great sum from all his people he had got nearly as much from the Jews as from his Christian subjects. From the former he got a fourth of their property, £60,000, from the latter a tenth, or £70,000.[3] It is of course improbable that, as these figures would at first seem to show, the Jews held a quarter of the wealth of the kingdom, but

[1] Radulfi de Diceto, *Opera Historica* (R.S.), II. 75-6.   Jacobs, *Jews of Angevin England*, 176; *Chronicles of the Reigns of Stephen, Henry II., and Richard I.* (Rolls Series), I. 309-10, 312-322.

[2] *Chronicles of the Reigns of Stephen, Henry II., and Richard I.* (R.S.) I. 323-4.

[3] Jacobs, *Jews of Angevin England*. pp. 91-6; Gervase of Canterbury (.S.) I. 422.

they were as useful to the King as if they had. He had a far greater power over their resources than over those of his other subjects; their wealth was in moveable property, and what was still more important, it was concentrated in few hands. It was easily found and easily taken away.[1]

II.—THE CONSTITUTION OF THE JEWRY.

Richard's policy, or his councillors', was simple. On the one hand, in order to encourage rich Jews to continue to make England their home, he issued a charter of protection, in which he guaranteed to certain Jews,[2] and perhaps to all who were wealthy, the privileges that they had enjoyed under his father and great-grandfather. They were to hold land as they had hitherto done; their heirs were to succeed to their money debts; they were to be allowed to go wherever they pleased throughout the country, and to be free of all tolls and dues. On the other hand he asserted and enforced his rights over them and their property by organising a complete supervision of all their business transactions. In 1194 he issued a code of regulations, in which he ordered that a register of all that belonged to them should be kept for the information of the treasury. All their deeds were to be executed in one of the six or seven places where there were establishments of Jewish and Christian clerks especially appointed to witness them; they were to be entered on an official list, and a half of each was to be deposited in a public chest under the control of royal officers.[3] No Jew was to plead before any court but that of the King's officers, and special Justices were appointed

---

[1] Enormous wealth was possessed by Abraham fil Rabbi, Jurnet of Norwich and Aaron of Lincoln.   Jacobs. *Op. Cit.*, 14, 64, 84, 90, 91.

[2] Rymer, *Fœdera* I. 51.

[3] *Chronica Rogeri de Hoveden* (R.S.), III. 266-7.

to hear cases in which Jews were concerned, and to
exercise a general control over their business.[1]

These arrangements underwent various modifications
under Richard's successors. The privileges which had at
first been granted to certain Jews by name were extended
by John to the whole community[2]; and the royal hold
over them was tightened by an edict, issued in 1210, which
ordered the Wardens of the Cinque Ports to prevent any
Jews who lived in England from leaving the country.[3]

This elaborate constitution did not indeed afford complete security against a repetition of the massacres of 1189
and 1190, but its existence was a more solemn and official
recognition than had been given before of the fact that
the King was the sole lord and protector of the Jews, and
that he would regard an injury done to them as an injury
to himself. And thus it went far to secure to him
his revenue and to them their safety. From this
time forward, the Jews yielded to the king, not
simply irregular contributions, such as the £60,000 they
had paid to Henry II., and the sums they had paid to Long-
champ towards the expenses of Richard's Crusade,[4] but a
steady and regular income. They paid tallages, heavy
reliefs on succeeding to property, and a besant in the
pound, or ten per cent., on their loan transactions; they
were liable to escheats, confiscation of land and debts, and
fines and amercements of all kinds.[5] Their average annual
contribution to the Treasury, during the latter part of the
twelfth century, was probably about a twelfth of the whole
Royal revenue,[6] and of the greater part of what they owed
the realisation was nearly certain. Other debtors might
find in delay, or resistance, or legal formalities, a way of

[1] *Chronicon Johannis Brompton* in Twysden's *Historiæ Anglicanæ
Scriptores* X., col. 1258.

[2] *Rotuli Chartarum* (Record Commission), p. 93.

[3] Tovey. *Anglia Judaica*, 81.

[4] *Gesta Henrici II. et Ricard. I.* (R.S.), II. 218; M. Paris. *Chronica
Majora* (R.S.) II. 381. and Jacobs. 162-4.

[5] Jacobs. 222, 228-30, 239-40.   [6] *Ibid.* 328.

avoiding payment. But the King had the Jews in his own
hands. He could order the sheriffs of the county to distrain
on defaulters, and there was no one between the sheriffs
and the Jews.[1] He could despoil them of lands and debts.
He could imprison them in the royal castles. In the reign
of John, all the Jews and Jewesses of England were thrown
into prison by his command, and are said to have been
reduced to such poverty that they begged from door to
door, and prowled about the city like dogs.[2] The only
way they had of removing any of their property from his
reach was by burying it. Whereupon the King, if he
suspected that a Jew had more treasure than was apparent,
might order him to have a tooth drawn every day until
he paid enough to purchase pardon.[3]

Powerless as the Jews were against royal oppression in
England, the position that was offered to them by Richard
and John was no worse than that of their co-religionists
in other countries of Europe. Those of Germany were the
Emperor's *Kammerknechte*;[4] those of France had been
expelled in 1182, and though they were soon recalled, might
at any time be expelled again.[5] A Jew in a feudalised
country was liable to be the subject of quarrel between the
lord on whose estate he dwelt and the king of the country,
and he could be handed about, now to the one and now to
the other.[6] The right to live and to be under jurisdiction, was
everywhere still a local privilege that had to be enjoyed by
the permission of a lord, lay or clerical, and had to be paid for.
In England, the Jews, so long as they were protected by
the King, were at any rate under the greatest lord in

[1] Jacobs, 222.

[2] M. Paris, *Chronica Majora* (R.S.) II. 528 ; *Annales Monastici* (R.S.)
I. 29, II. 264. III. 32, 451 ; *Chronicles of Lanercost* (Maitland Club), p. 7.

[3] M. Paris, *Chronica Majora* II., 528.

[4] Depping. *Les Juifs dans le Moyen Age*, 185.

[5] Bouquet. *Recueil des Historiens des Gaules et de la France*, xvii. 9.

[6] Depping, *Les Juifs dans le Moyen Age*, 59. 60. 185, 191. Cf. *Rotuli
Chartarum*, I. 75 (*Carta Willielmi Marescalli, de quodam Judaeo apud
Cumbay*).

the land. The towns where especially they wished to settle for the purposes of their business, were, thanks to the policy of William the Conqueror, mostly on the royal domain. And the royal power acting through its local officers was used to the full to protect the Jews. The sheriffs of the counties were especially charged to secure to them personal safety and the enjoyment of the immunities that had been granted to them.[1]

The arrangement by which Jewish money-lenders received on English soil the protection of the King against his own subjects was not very honourable to either of the parties. But the King had no compunction, and the Jews had no choice. It could endure so long as the royal power was strong enough to override the objections of barons and abbots to a measure in favour of their creditors, of the towns to an encroachment on their privileges, and of the Church to the royal support of a body of infidel usurers.

At the end of the twelfth century neither towns nor landholders nor Church were in a position to offer any effectual protest. In the thirteenth century the strength of the opposition of each of these three orders grew steadily. But in each it pursued a separate course, though to the same end, and each order struck its decisive blow at a different moment. Hence the various forms of opposition must be separately considered.

III.—The Conflict with the Towns.

The towns were the first to carry out a practical and effective anti-Jewish policy. It was they that suffered most keenly and constantly from the presence of the Jews. They had bought, at great expense, from King or noble or abbot, the right to be independent, self-governing communities, living under the jurisdiction of their own

---

[1] Tovey. *Anglia Judaica*, 78-9.

officers, free from the visits of the royal sheriffs, and paying
a fixed sum in commutation of all dues to the King or the
local lord; and yet many of them saw the King protecting
in their midst a band of foreigners, who had the royal permission to go whithersoever they pleased, who could dwell
among the burgesses, and were yet free not only from all
customs and dues and contribution to the ferm,[1] but even
from the jurisdiction of those authorities which were responsible for peace and good government.[2] This was exasperat-
ing enough; but there was more and worse. The exclusion
of the sheriff and the King's constables was one of the
most cherished privileges of towns, but, wherever the
Jews had once taken up their residence, it was in danger
of being a mere pretence. At Colchester, if a Jew was
unable to recover his debts, he could call in the King's
sheriffs to help him. In London, Jews were "warrantised"
from the exchequer, and the constable of the Tower had
a special jurisdiction by which he kept the pleas between
Jews and Christians. At Nottingham, complaints against
Jews, even in cases of petty assaults, were heard before
the keeper of the Castle. At Oxford the constable called
in question the Chancellor's authority over the Jews;
contending that they did not form part of the ordinary
town-community.[3] Moreover, the debts of the Jews were
continually falling into the King's hands, and whenever
this happened, his officers would no doubt penetrate into

---

[1] Stamford was an exception in this respect, Madox, *Firma Burgi*
p. 182.

[2] Et Judæi non intrabunt in placitum nisi coram nobis aut coram illis,
qui turres nostras custodierint in quorum ballivis Judæi manserint,
Rot. Chart., 93.

[3] Cutts, *Colchester*, 123; Tovey, *Anglia J.*, 50; *Forty-Seventh Report
of Deputy-Keeper of Public Records*, 306; Lyte, *History of the University of Oxford*, 59; *Papers of Anglo-Jewish Historical Exhibition*,
35-6; *De Antiquis Legibus Liber* (Camden Soc.), p. 16. (A.D. 1249, Nam
rex concessit quod Judei qui antea warantizati fuerunt per breve de
scaccario, de cetero placitassent coram civibus de tenementis suis in
Londoniis). *Chronica Jocelini de Brakelonda* (Camden Soc.), p. 2, (Venit
Judeus portans literas domini regis de debito sacristæ).

the town to make on behalf of the royal treasury a collection such as had never been contemplated when the burgesses made their agreement, which was to settle once and for all their payment to the King.[1]

In some of the towns the feeling against the Jews was expressed in riots as early as the reign of John, and the beginning of that of Henry III. But the King in each case took stern measures of repression. John told the mayor and barons of London that he should require the blood of the Jews at their hands if any ill befell them.[2] In Gloucester and in Hereford, the burgesses of the town were made responsible for the safety of the Jews dwelling amongst them. In Worcester, York, Lincoln, Stamford, Bristol, Northampton, and Winchester, the sheriffs were charged with the duty of protecting them against injury.[3] Such measures only increased the ill-feeling of the burgesses. At Norwich in 1234 the Jewry was fired and looted.[4] The Jews were maltreated and beaten, and were only saved from further harm by the timely help of the garrison of the neighbouring castle. At Oxford the scholars attacked the Jewry and carried off "innumerable goods."[5]

But the towns soon began to use a far more effective method than rioting in order to rid themselves of the Jews. Just as they had found it worth while to pay heavily for their municipal charters, so now they were willing to pay more for a measure which would secure them in the future against a drain on their revenues and a violation of their privileges. Whether a town held its

---

[1] Cp. *Chronica Monasterii de Melsa* (R.S.). I., 177. Interea mortuus est Aaron Judæus Lincolniæ, de quo jam dictum est, et compulsi sumus, regis edicto totum quod illi debuimus pro Willielmo Fossard infra breve tempus domino regi persolvere.

[2] Rymer. *Fœdera*, I., 89.

[3] *Calendar of Patent Rolls from* 1281 to 1292, p. 15 ; Tovey, *Anglia Judaica*, 77, 78, 79.

[4] Tovey, 101, *Norfolk Antiquarian Miscellany*, I., 326.

[5] *Annales Monastici* (Rolls Series), iv. 91.

charter from the King, or was still dependent on an intermediate lord, the motive was equally strong. An abbot or a baron would be glad to second the efforts made by the inhabitants of one of his vills to expel a portion of the populace which took much from the resources whence his revenue came and added nothing to them.[1] The abbot of Bury St. Edmund's induced the King to expel the Jews from the town in 1190.[2] The burgesses of Leicester obtained a similar grant from Simon de Montfort in 1231, those of Newcastle in 1234, of Wycombe in 1235, of Southampton in 1236, of Berkhampsted in 1242, of Newbury in 1244, of Derby in 1263; at Norwich the citizens complained to the King, but without any result, of the harm that they suffered through the growth of the Jewish community settled in the city.[3] In 1245 a decree in general terms was issued by Henry III., prohibiting all Jews, except those to whom the King had granted a special personal license, from remaining in any town other than those in which their co-religionists had hitherto been accustomed to live.[4] This series of measures did not simply deprive the Jews in England of a right which had been solemnly granted them and which they had long enjoyed. It went much further.

---

[1] Especially irritating must have been the fact that the one restriction on the business of Jews, as money-lenders, was the order that forbade them to take in pledge the land of tenants on the royal demesne. W. Prynne, *The Second Part of a Short Demurrer to the Jews' long discontinued remitter*, etc., London, 1656, p. 35 ; *Norfolk Antiquarian Miscellany*, I. 328.

[2] *Chronica Jocelini de Brakelonda* (Camden Society), p. 33.

[3] Thompson, *Leicester*, 72 ; Madox, *Hist. of Exchequer*, I. 260, notes O and P ; J. E. Blunt, *Establishment and Residence of Jews in England*, 45 ; Papers Anglo-J. II. Ex. 190 ; Prynne, *The Second Part of a Short Demurrer*, etc., p. 37 ; *Norfolk Antiquarian Miscellany*, I. 326. (De Judeis dicebant quod major multitudo manet in civitate sua quam solebat, et quod Judei qui aliis locis dissainati (*sic*) faerunt venerunt ibidem manere ad dampnum civitatis).

[4] Prynne, *The Second Part of a Short Demurrer*, etc., p. 75 ; Madox, *History of the Exchequer*, I. 249 : Et quod nullus Judaeus receptetur in aliqua villa sine speciali licentia Regis, nisi in villis illis in quibus Judaei manere consueverunt.

For, by circumscribing the area in which they could carry on their business, and so diminishing their opportunities of acquiring wealth, it threatened their very existence in a land where their wealth alone secured them protection.

IV.—THE CONFLICT WITH THE BARONS.

At the same time that the towns were making their attack on the Jews in their own way, there was growing up within the baronial order a new party, stronger than the towns in the elements of which it was composed and in its capacity for joint action, and filled, on account of the private circumstances of its members, with a deeper hatred of the Jews than the greater barons, who had hitherto represented the order, had ever known. For the old Baronial party which had forced Magna Carta on John was too rich to be seriously indebted to the Jews, and the anti-Jewish feeling of its members must have been blunted by the fact that, when they had to pay their debts, they could raise the money by benevolences levied on their tenants.[1] Moreover some of them imitated on their own estates the King's policy of sharing in the profits of usury.[2] Hence they were little influenced by personal grievances, and it was no doubt partly from political considerations, and partly as a concession to the lesser and poorer members of their order, that they had introduced into Magna Carta certain limitations of the power of the Jews, or of their legatee, the King, over the estates of

[1] Jacobs, *Jews of Angevin England*, 269-271.
[2] M. Paris, *Chronica Majora*, V. 245. Cf. the article in the Constitutions enacted by Walter de Cantilupe, Bishop of Worcester, at his diocesan synod in 1240 : Quia vero parum refert, an quis per se vel per alium incidat in crimen usurarum, prohibemus ne quis Christianus Judæo pecuniam committat, ut eam Judæus simulate suo nomine proprio mutuet ad usuram. Wilkins. *Magnæ Britanniæ Concilia*, I. 675,676. Stubbs, *Select Charters*, 385-6.

debtors, a measure which, small as it was, was repealed on
the re-issues of the charters, when, during the minority of
Henry III., the great Barons had to undertake the duty
of Government. And yet even the great Barons must have
felt, after twenty years' experience of the personal Government of Henry III., that an alteration in the Royal system of
managing the Jewry was necessary if their order was ever
to succeed in the constitutional struggle in which it was
engaged. They knew that many of those among the King's
acts which they hated worst would have been impossible
but for the Jews. It was by money extorted from them
that he had been enabled to prolong his expeditions in
Brittany and Gascony, to support and enrich his foreign
favourites, and to baffle the attempts of the Council to
secure, by the refusal of supplies, the restoration of Government through the customary officers. In 1230, and again in
1239, he took from them a third of their property; in 1244,
he levied a tallage of 60,000 marks; in 1250, 1252, 1254,
and 1255 he ordered the royal officers to take from them
all that they could exact, after thorough inquisition and the
employment of measures of compulsion so cruel as to make
the whole body of Jews in England ask twice, though
each time in vain, for permission to leave the country.
Thus the whole Baronial order was for a time united, on
the ground of constitutional grievances, in a policy which
found its expression in the successful attempt of the
National Council in 1244 to exact from the King the right
of appointing one of the two justices of the Jews, so as to
gain a knowledge of the amount of the Jewish revenue,
and a power of controlling its expenditure.[1]

---

[1] For the nature and duration of the earlier struggle between the king
and the barons, see Stubbs, *Constitutional History of England* (Library
Edition), II., 40, 44, 63, 67, 69-77. For the king's acts of extortion from
the Jews, see Matthew Paris, *Chronica Majora*, III., 194, 543; IV., 88;
V., 114, 274, 441, 487; Madox, *History of the Exchequer*, I., 224-5, 229;
Prynne, *Second Part of a Short Demurrer*, 40, 48, 66, 70, 75, 57. For the
appointment by the Council of one Justice of the Jews, M. Paris, *Chronica
Majora*, iv. 367.

But such a measure did nothing to relieve the personal grievances of the lower baronage, and it was naturally from this class that further complaints proceeded. Its members, unlike the greater barons, made no profit from the encouragement of usury. On the other hand, they were among the greatest sufferers from the practice. Many a one among them must, when summoned to take part in the King's foreign expeditions, have been compelled to pledge some land to the Jews in order to be able to meet the expenses of service; and no doubt the Jews derived from such transactions a large share of the profits that enabled them to make their enormous contributions to the exchequer. A landholder's debt to a Jew would, when once contracted, have been, under any circumstances, difficult to pay off. But the lower baronage, or knight's bachelors, were threatened, when they had fallen into debt, with new dangers, the knowledge of which intensified their hatred of the whole system of money-lending. "We ask," they said in the petition of 1259, "a remedy for this evil, to wit, that the Jews sometimes give their bonds, and the land pledged to them, to the magnates and the more powerful men of the realm, who thereupon enter on the land of the lesser men, and although those who owe the debt be willing to pay it with usury, yet the said magnates put off the business, so that the land and tenements may in some way remain their property, ... and on the occasion of death, or any other chance, there is a manifest danger that those to whom the said tenements belonged may lose all right in them."[1]

The special wrongs of the lower baronage were, in the course of the Civil War, temporarily lost sight of. Nevertheless, the action of the whole baronial party throughout the war contributed greatly, though indirectly, to the ultimate banishment of the Jews from England. Just as the

---

[1] Stubbs, *Select Charters*, 385-6.

towns had, by their measures of exclusion, weakened the mercenary bond that united the Jews to the King, so now the barons, by their wholesale destruction of Jewish property, worked, as unconsciously as the towns had done, to the same end. They attacked and plundered the Jewry of London twice in the course of the war, and destroyed those of Canterbury, Northampton, Winchester, Cambridge, Worcester, and Lincoln. Everywhere they carried off or destroyed the property of their victims. In London they killed every Jew that they met, except those who accepted baptism, or paid large sums of money. They took from Cambridge all the Jewish bonds that were kept there, and deposited them at their head-quarters in Ely. At Lincoln they broke open the official chests, and "trod underfoot in the lanes, charters and deeds, and whatever else was injurious to the Christians."[1] "It is impossible," says a chronicler, in describing one of these attacks, "to estimate the loss it caused to the King's exchequer."

V.—THE BEGINNING OF EDWARD'S POLICY OF RESTRICTION.

When the Civil War was over, the position of the King's son Edward as, on the one hand, the sworn friend of the lower baronage, and, on the other hand, the leader of the Council and the most powerful man in England,[2] made it impossible that the Jews should continue to carry on their business under the royal protection as they had hitherto done. And Edward's personal character and political ideals were such as to make him execute with vigour the policy

---

[1] *Annales Monastici,* II. 101, 363, 371, III. 230, IV. 141, 142, 145, 449, 450 ; *Liber de Antiquis Legibus* (Camden Society), 62 ; *Chronicle of Pierre de Langtoft* (R. S.), II., 151 ; *Chronicle of William de Rishanger* (Camden Society). 21, 25, 126 ; *Florentii Wigorniensis Chronicon ex Chronicis* (English Historical Society), II. 192.

Tout, *Edward I.,* 13, 39.

towards the Jews that was forced on him by his relations
with the lower baronage. He was a religious prince, one
who could not but feel qualms of conscience at seeing
the " enemies of Christ " carrying on the most unchristian
trade of usury in the chief towns of England. He was
a statesman, the future author of the Statutes of Mort-
main and *Quia Emptores*, and he wished to see the work of
the nation performed by the united action of the nation,
and its expenses met by due contributions from all the
National resources. But in so far as the Jews had any
hold on English land they prevented the realisation of this
ideal. Sometimes they took possession of land that was
pledged to them, and then the amount of the feudal revenue and the symmetry of the feudal organisation suffered,
though the King might gain a great deal in other ways;[1]
very often they secured payment in money of their debts
by bringing about an agreement for the transfer to a
monastery of the estates that had been pledged to them as
security,[2] and then the land came under the " dead hand ";
sometimes they contented themselves with a perpetual
rent-charge,[3] and then it would be hard, if not impossible,
for the struggling debtor to discharge his feudal obligations.[4]

The indebtedness of the Church must have shocked
Edward's sympathies as a Christian, just as much as the
indebtedness of the lay landholders thwarted his schemes

---

[1] Palgrave, *Rotuli Curiæ Regis* (Record Commission), II.. 62 (Judaei
habeant seisinam) ; *Gesta abbatum Monasterii S. Albani* (R. S.), I., 401 ;
Placitorum Abbreviatio (Record Commission), p. 58 ; Jacobs, pp. 90, 234.

[2] *Chronicles of the Abbey of Melsa* (Rolls Series), I., 173, 174, 306. 367,
374, 377 ; II., 55, 109, 116 ; *Archæological Journal*, vol. 38, pp. 189. 190,
191, 192.

[3] Blunt, *Establishment and Residence of the Jews in England*, 136 ;
Prynne, *Second Part of a Short Demurrer*, p. 105.

[4] A very long list of landowners indebted to the Jews could be ex-
tracted from Madox, *History of Exchequer*, Vol. I., p. 227. *sq.* Cf. Prynne,
Second Part, etc., pp. 96, 98, 106 ; *Calendar of Patent Rolls from* 1281
to 1292. p. 25.

as a statesman. For the condition of ecclesiastical estates was indeed deplorable. They had begun to fall into debt in the twelfth century, no doubt in consequence of the expense that was necessary for the erection of great buildings, and their debts had gone on growing, partly in consequence of bad management, partly through the necessity of fulfilling the duties of hospitality by keeping open house continually, partly through the exactions of the Pope and the King. The Bishop of Lincoln pledged the plate of his cathedral, the Abbot of Peterborough the bones of the patron-saint of his Abbey; at Bury St. Edmunds each obedientiary had his own seal, which he could apply to bonds which involved the whole house; and loans were freely contracted which accumulated at 50 per cent.[1] Hence in the thirteenth century Matthew Paris wrote that "there was scarcely anyone in England, especially a bishop, who was not caught in the meshes of the usurers."[2] "Wise men knew that the land was corrupted by them."[3] The literary documents of the latter half of the century fully confirm these accounts. The See of Canterbury was weighed down with an ever-growing load of debt when John of Peckham first went to it.[4] The buildings of the cathedral were becoming dilapidated for want of money to repair them.[5] Those of the neighbouring Priory of Christ Church were in an equally bad state, and its revenue was equally encumbered.[6] The bishop of Norwich was so poor that in spite of the extortions regularly practised by his officials, he had to borrow six hundred marks from the Archbishop of Canterbury.[7] The Bishop of Hereford had been compelled to seek the intervention of Henry III., in order to obtain respite of his debts to

---

[1] *Gesta Henrici II.* (R. S.), I., 106 ; *Giraldi Cambrensis Opera* (R. S.), VII., 36 ; *Cronica Jocelini de Brakelonda* (Camden Soc.), p. 2.

III., 328.   [3] V. 189.

Letters of John of Peckham (Rolls Series), I., 20, 156,

[5] *Ibid.*, I., 203.   [6] *Ibid.*, I., 341.

[7] *Ibid.*, I., 177, 187.

the Jews.[1] The Abbey of Glastonbury was weighed down by "immeasurable debts," and, in order to save it from further calamities, the Archbishop had to order a reorganisation of expenditure so thorough as to include regulations concerning the number of dishes with which the abbot might be served in his private room.[2] The Prior of Lewes asked permission to turn one of his churches from its right use, and to let it for five years to any one who would hire it, in order that he might thus get together some money to help to pay off what the priory owed.[3] The Church of Newneton could not afford clergymen.[4] Even the great Monastery of St. Swithin's, Winchester, in spite of the revenue that its monks drew from the sale of wine and fur and spiceries, and from the tolls paid by the traders who attended its great annual fair, was always in debt, sometimes to the amount of several thousand pounds.[5] Except in the cutting down of timber and the granting of life annuities in return for the payment of a lump sum, the religious houses had no resources except the money-lenders.[6] They borrowed from English usurers, from Italians, from Jews, and from one another.[7]

If the lay and ecclesiastical estates of England were to be freed from their burdens, heroic measures were necessary. The barons had done their part in the work by carrying off or destroying such bonds as they could find. But the financial revolution, to be effective, must be carried out by due process of law.

When, on the restoration of tranquillity, the Council under Edward's influence began its attempt to redress the grievances against which the barons had been fighting, the

---

[1] Roberts. *Excerpta e Rot. Finium* (Record Commission), II., 68.
[2] *Letters of John of Peckham*, I., 261.   [3] *Ibid.*, I., 380.
[4] *Ibid.*, I., 194.
[5] *Obedientiary Rolls of S. Swithin's, Winchester* (Hampshire Record Society), 1892, pp. 10, 18.
[6] *Letters of John of Peckham*, I., 244; Kitchin, *Winchester*, 55; *Obedientiary Rolls of S. Swithin's*, pp. 22, 25.
[7] Cf. *Letters of John of Peckham*, I., 512.

first measure in the programme of reform was one for the relief of the debtors of the Jews. Any interference with Jewish business would, of course, entail a loss to the Royal Exchequer, and, honest and patriotic as Edward was, his poverty was so great that he could not afford to sacrifice any of his resources. But the exhausting demands that the King had made on the Jews in the time of his difficulties, and the terrible destruction of their property that had taken place during the war, must have so far diminished the revenue to be derived from the Jews as to make the possible loss of it a far less serious consideration than it would have been twenty years earlier. Accordingly, at the feast of St. Hilary in 1269, a measure, drawn up by Walter of Merton, was passed, forbidding for the future the alienation of land to Jews in consequence of loan transactions All existing bonds by which land might pass into the hands of Jews were declared cancelled ; the attempt to evade the law by selling them to Christians was made punishable with death and forfeiture ; and none to such effect was to be executed in future.[1]

But this was only a slight measure compared with what was to follow. The Jews might still acquire land by purchase, and needy lords and churches, when forbidden to pledge their lands, were very likely, under the pressure of necessity, to sell them outright. Already the Jews were " seised " of many estates,[2] and, according to the story of an ancient historian,[3] they chose this moment to ask the King to grant them the enjoyment of the privileges that regularly accompanied the possession of land, viz., the guardianship of minors on their estates, the right to give wards in marriage, and the presentation to livings. Feudal law recognised the two former privileges, and the

---

[1] Tovey, *Anglia Judaica*, 175-7.

[2] *Gesta Abbatum Monasterii S. Albani* (Rolls Series), I. 401 ; *Placitorum Abbreviatio* (Record Commission), p. 58, col. 2.

[3] *De Antiquis Legibus Liber* (Camden Society), 234 *sq.*

Church recognised the latter,[1] as incidental to the possession
of real property.   It was strange, however, that the Jews
should present a demand for new social privileges of this
kind to a council that had already shown its determination
to deprive them of their old legal rights; and it was only
natural that the churchmen should take the opportunity
of denouncing their "impious insolence." Certain of the
councillors were at first in favour of granting the Jews'
request ; but a Franciscan friar, who obtained admittance
to the Council, pleaded that it would be a disgrace to
Christianity, and a dishonour to God.   The Archbishop of
York, and the Bishops of Lichfield, Coventry, and Worcester
were present, and argued that the "perfidious Jews" ought
to be made to recognise that it was as an act of the King's
grace that they were allowed to remain in England, and
that it was outrageous that they should make a demand,
the granting of which would allow them to nominate the
ministers of Christian churches, to receive the homage of
Christians, to sit side by side with them on juries, assizes
and recognitions, and perhaps ultimately to come into
possession of English baronies.   Edward and his equally
religious cousin, the son of Richard, King of the Romans,
were present at the council to support the argument of the
Bishops,[2] and not only were the original requests refused,
but the Jews were now forbidden by the act of the King
and his Council to enjoy a freehold in "manors, lands,
tenements, fiefs, rents, or tenures of any kind," whether
held by bond, gift, enfeoffment, confirmation, or any other
grant, or by any other means whatever.   They were forbidden to receive any longer the rent-charges which
had been a common form of security for their loans.
Lands of which they were already possessed were to
be redeemed by the Christian owners, or in default of
them, by other Christians, on repayment without interest

---

[1] Hefele. *Conciliengeschichte.* V., 1028.

[2] *Annales Monastici* (R.S.). IV., 221.

of the principal of the loan in consequence of which they
had come into the hands of the Jews. In the interest
of parochial revenues, Jews were forbidden to acquire
houses in London in addition to those which they already
possessed.[1]

VI.—THE PROHIBITION OF USURY.

Very soon after the passing of the Statute of 1270,
Edward left England to join the second Crusade of St.
Louis, and did not return till 1274, two years after he
had been proclaimed king. At once he took up with
characteristic vigour, and with the help and advice of a
band of statesmen and lawyers, the work of administrative
reform that he had already begun as heir-apparent. He
recognised that the state of affairs established in 1270
could not endure, since, under it, the Jews, while practically prevented from lending money at interest, now that
the law forbade them to take in pledge real property, the
only possible security for large loans, were nevertheless
still nothing but usurers, allowed by ancient custom and
royal recognition to carry on that one pursuit as best they
could, and prevented by the same forces from carrying on
any other. Edward, with his usual love for "the defini-
tion of duties and the spheres of duty,"[2] felt that it was
necessary to define for the Jews a new position, which
should not, as did their present position, condemn them
to hopeless struggles, nor demand from him acquiescence
in what he believed to be a sin.

For the Church had never ceased to maintain the
doctrine of the sinfulness of usury which Ambrose and
Clement, Jerome and Tertullian, had taught in strict
conformity with the communistic ideas of primitive
Christianity. It is true that till the eleventh century

[1] Blunt, *Establishment and Residence*, etc., 134-9.
[2] Stubbs, *Constitutional History*. II., 116.

usury and speculative trading generally had not been
active enough to call for repression, nor would the Church
have been strong enough to enforce on the Christian world
the observance of its doctrine. It could not follow up
the attempt made by the Capitularies of Charles the Great
to prevent laymen from practising usury, and it had to
rest content with enforcing the prohibition on clerics.[1]
But the growth under Hildebrand of the power of the
Church over every-day life, and the elevation of the moral
tone of its teaching that resulted from its struggles with
the temporal power, enabled it to adopt with increasing
effect measures of greater severity. Hildebrand, in 1083,
decreed that usurers should, like perjurers, thieves, and
wife-deserters, be punished with excommunication;[2] and
the Lateran General Council of 1139, when exhorted by
Innocent II. to shrink from no legislation as demanding
too high and rigorous a morality, decreed that usurers
were to be excluded from the consolations of the Church,
to be infamous all their lives long, and to be deprived of
Christian burial.[3] The religious feeling aroused by the
Crusades still further strengthened the hold on the
Christian world of characteristically Christian theory,
while the prospect of the economic results that they
threatened to bring about in Europe, awoke the Church
to the advisability of putting forth all its power to
protect the estates of Crusaders against the money-lenders.
Many Popes of the twelfth century ordained, and St.
Bernard approved of the ordinance [4] that those who took
up the Cross should be freed from all engagements to
pay usury into which they might have entered. Innocent
III. absolved Crusaders even from obligations of the kind
that they had incurred under oath, and subsequently
ordered that Jews should be forced, under penalty of

---

[1] Ashley, *Economic History and Theory*, I., 126-32, 148-50.

[2] Hefele, *Conciliengeschichte*, V., 175.

[3] *Ibid.*, 438-441.   [4] Jacobs, *The Jews of Angevin England*. 23.

exclusion from the society of Christians, to return to
their crusading debtors any interest that they had already
received from them.[1]

Stronger even than the influence of the Crusades was
that of the Mendicant Orders. The Dominicans, who
preached, and the Franciscans, who "taught and wrought"
among all classes of people throughout Europe, carried with
them, as their most cherished lesson, the doctrine of poverty.
It was by the teaching of this doctrine, and by the practice
of the simple unworldly life of the primitive Church, that
the founders of the two orders had been able to give new
strength to the ecclesiastical institutions of the thirteenth
century. And their teaching, if not their practice, made
its way from the Casiuncula to the Vatican. Cardinal
Ugolino, the dear friend of S. Francis, became Gregory
IX.; Petrus de Tarentagio, of the order of the Dominicans,
became Innocent IV.; and Girolamo di Ascoli, the "sun"
of the Franciscans, was soon to become Nicholas IV.
Moreover, the work of formulating and publishing to the
world the official doctrines of the Church was in the
hands of the Mendicants. A Dominican, Raymundus de
Peñaforte, was entrusted by Gregory IX. with the
preparation of the Decretals, which formed the chief
part of the canon law of the Church.[2]   And friars of
both orders codified with indefatigable labour the moral
law of Christianity, and set it forth in hand-books, or
Summæ, which were universally accepted as guides for
the confessional, and which all agreed in condemning
usury.[3]   Hence, the doctrine of its sinfulness was taught
throughout Christian Europe, by priests and monks, by
Dominican preachers and Franciscan confessors, who could
enforce their lesson by the use of their power of granting

[1] *Corpus Juris Canonici* (Leipzig, 1839), II., 786.
[2] Raumer, *Geschichte der Hohenstaufen und ihrer Zeit*, III., 581.
[3] Endemann, *Studien in der Romanisch-Kanonistischen Wirthschafts-und Rechtslehre*, I., 16-18. Stintzing, *Geschichte der Populären Literatur des Römisch-Canonischen Rechts*.

or refusing absolution. How strong and violent a public opinion was thus created is best shown in the lines in which Dante, the contemporary of Edward I., tells with what companions he thought it fit that the Caursine usurers should dwell in hell.[1]

There was every reason why the hatred of usury should be as strong in England as anywhere. The Franciscan movement had spread throughout the country, and had found among Englishmen many of its chief literary champions.[2] And the Englishman's pious dislike of usury had been strengthened by many years of bitter experience. Italian usurers had in the previous reign gone up and down the country collecting money on behalf of the Pope, and lending money on their own account at exorbitant rates of interest.[3] From some of the magnates they obtained protection (for which they are said to have paid with a share of their profits),[4] but to the great body of the Baronage, to the Church, and to the trading classes their very name had become hateful. One of them, the brother of the Pope's Legate, had been killed at Oxford.[5] In London Bishop Roger had solemnly excommunicated them all, and excluded them from his diocese.[6]

No English king who wished to follow the teachings of Christianity could willingly countenance any of his subjects in carrying on a traffic which was thus hated by the people and condemned by all the doctors of Christendom Even Henry III. was once so far moved by indignation and religious feeling as to expel the Caursines from his kingdom,[7] and had religious scruples about the retention of the Jews.[8] But, as has been shown, he could not do with-

---

[1] E pero lo minor giron suggella,
Del segno suo e Sodoma e Caorsa.
　　　　　　　　　Inferno, XI. 49, 50.
[2] *Monumenta Franciscana* (Rolls Series), XLV., L., 10, 38-9, 61.
[3] Macpherson, *Annals of Commerce*, I., 399-400.
[4] M. Paris, *Chronica Majora*, V., 245.　[5] *Ibid.*, III., 44.
[6] *Ibid.*, III., 332-3.　　　　　　[7] *Ibid.*, IV., 5.
[8] M. Paris, *Historia Anglorum*, III., 104.

out the Jewish revenue. Edward was not only free from dependence on that source of income, but he was also a far more religious king than his father. He was a man to obey the behests of the Church, instead of setting them at naught with an easy conscience, as his father had done. In the second year of his reign the Church, by a decree passed at the Council of Lyons, demanded from the Christian world far greater efforts against usury than ever before.[1] Till this time, though Popes and Councils had declared the practice accursed, churches and monasteries had had usurers as tenants on their estates, or had even possessed whole ghettos as their property.[2] Now this was to be ended, and it was ordained by Gregory X. that no community, corporation, or individual should permit foreign usurers to hire their houses, or indeed to dwell at all upon their lands, but should expel them within three months. Edward, in obedience to this decree, ordered an inquisition to be made into the usury of the Florentine bankers in his kingdom with a view to its suppression, and allowed proceedings to be taken at the same time and with the same object against a citizen of London.[3] And the events of the last reign enabled him to proceed to what at first seems the far more serious task of bringing to an end the trade that the Jews had carried on under the patronage, and for the benefit, of the Royal Exchequer.

For the Jews could no longer support the Crown in times of financial difficulty as they had been able to do in previous reigns. The contraction of their business that

---

[1] Ashley, *Economic History and Theory*, I. 150 ; Labbeus, *Sacrosancta Concilia*, xi. 991, 2.

[2] Depping, *Les Juifs dans le Moyen Age*, 202, 207 ; Muratori, *Antiquitates Italicæ Medii Aevi*, I. 899, 900 ; *Ninth Report of the Historical Manuscripts Commission*, p. 14 (No. 264).

[3] *Forty-fourth Report of Deputy-Keeper of Public Records*, pp. 8, 9, 72 ; *The Question whether a Jew*, etc., by a Gentleman of Lincoln's Inn (London, 1753), Appendix, § 18.

was the result of their exclusion from many towns, and the losses that they had suffered through the extortions of Henry III. and the plundering attacks of the barons, had very greatly diminished their revenue-paying capacities, and the legislation of 1270 must have affected them still more deeply. At the end of the twelfth century they had probably paid to the Treasury about £3,000 a year, or one-twelfth of the whole royal income,[1] and for some parts of the thirteenth century the average collection of tallage has been estimated at £5,000 ;[2] but in 1271—by which time the royal income had probably grown to something like the £65,000 a year which the Edwards are said to have enjoyed in time of peace[3]—Henry III., when pledging to Richard of Cornwall the revenue from the Jewry, estimated its annual value, apart from what was yielded by escheats and other special claims, at no more than 2,000 marks.[4] And while the resources of the Jews had fallen off, the needs of the Crown had increased. Not only must Edward have conducted his foreign enterprises at a much greater cost than did his predecessors, under whom the English knighthood had been accustomed to serve without serious opposition, but, in addition, he had to make the best of a vast heritage of debt that his father had left him.[5] He had to seek richer supporters than the Jews, and such were not wanting.

The Italian banking companies were the only organisations in Europe that could supply him with such sums of money as he needed. From all the greatest cities of Italy— from Florence, Rome, Milan, Pisa, Lucca, Siena, and Asti —they had spread to many of the chief countries of Europe,

---

[1] Jacobs. 328.   [2] *Papers Anglo-Jewish Hist. Exhibit.on*, 195.
[3] Stubbs' *Constitutional History*, II. 601.
[4] Rymer, *Foedera*, I. 489. Cf. *Jewish Chronicle* for April 26, 1895, p. 19, col. 2.
[5] *Chronicles Ed. I. and II.* (ed. Stubbs), Vol. I., p. c. Cf. *Forty-second Report of Deputy-Keeper of Public Records*, p. 479 (At the beginning of his reign Edward says, in his writs to the sheriffs, " Pecuniæ plurimam indigemus "). *Forty-third Report*, 419.

to France, England, Brabant, Switzerland, and Ireland.[1] They were merchants, money-leaders, money-changers, and international bankers, and in this last occupation their supremacy over all rivals was secured by the great advantage which the wide extent of their dealings enabled them to enjoy, of being able to save, by the use of letters of credit on their colleagues and countrymen, the cost of the transport of money from country to country.[2] They were thus the greatest financial agents of the time. They transacted the business of the Pope. At the Court of Rome ambassadors had to borrow from them.[3] In France their position was established by a regular diplomatic agreement between the head of their corporation and Philip III.[4] In England they had in their hands the greater part of the trade in corn and wool ;[5] and the protection and favour of English kings was often besought by the Popes on their behalf in special bulls.[6]

Edward began his reign in financial dependence on the Italians. His father had in the earliest period of his personal government incurred obligations to them which he himself, as heir apparent, had to increase considerably at the time of his Crusade.[7] When in later years he needed money to pay his army, he borrowed it from them ; when he diverted to his own use the tenth that was voted for his intended second Crusade, they gave security for repayment.[8] So great were the amounts that they advanced to him, that between 1298 and 1308 the Friscobaldi

---

[1] Muratori, *Antiquitates Italicæ Medii Ævi* (Dissertatio XVI); Depping, *Les Juifs dans le Moyen Age*, 213-6 ; Rymer, *Foedera*, I., 644.

[2] Macpherson, *Annals of Commerce*, I. 405, 6 ; and see Peruzzi, *Storia del Commercio e dei Banchieri di Firenze*, 170.

[3] Peruzzi, 169 ; *Archaeologia*, xxviii. 218, 219.

[4] Muratori, *Antiquitates Italicae Medii Ævi*, I. 889.

[5] *Archaeologia*, xxviii. 221 ; Cunningham, *Growth of English Industry and Commerce*, *Early and Middle Ages*, Appendix D ; Peruzzi, *Storia del Commercio*, 70.

[6] Rymer, *Foedera*, I. 660, 823, 905.

[7] *Archaeologia*, xxviii. 261-272.   [8] Rymer, *Foedera*, I. 644, 788.

Bianchi alone, one of the thirty-four companies that he employed,[1] received in repayment nearly £100,000.[2] He was compelled to favour them, although he attempted to stop their usury. He gave them a charter of privileges.[3] He presented them with large sums of money. He bestowed on the head of one of their firms high office in Gascony. At various times he placed under their charge the collection of the Customs in many of the chief ports in England.[4]

Edward's close connection with a body of financiers so rich and powerful made the Jews unnecessary to him. If he was not to disobey the decree of the Council of Lyons he must either withdraw his protection from them or else forbid them any longer to be usurers. To withdraw his protection from them would be to expose them to the popular hatred, the danger from which had been the justification of the relations that had been established between Crown and Jewry after 1190, and still existed. He chose the second alternative. In 1275 he issued a statute, in which he absolutely forbade the Jews, as he had just forbidden Christians,[5] to practise usury in the future. He gave warning that usurious contracts would no longer be enforced by the king's officers, and he declared the making of them to be an offence for which henceforth both parties were liable to punishment. To ensure that all those contracts already existing should come to an end as quickly as possible, he ordered that all movables that were in pledge on account of loans were to be redeemed before the coming Easter.[6]

VII.—EDWARD'S POLICY: THE JEWS AND TRADE.

Thus the Jews, already shut out from the feudal and municipal organisation of the country, were forbidden by

---

[1] Peruzzi, 174.   [2] *Archaeologia*, xxviii. 244-5.

[3] *Ibid*, 231, Note 1.   [4] Peruzzi, 172-5.

[5] *The Question whether a Jew*, etc.   Appendix, §18.   Prynne, *A Short Demurrer*, 58.   [6] Blunt, *Establishment and Residence*, etc., 139-141.

one act of legislation to follow the pursuit in which the kings of England had encouraged them for two hundred years.

However, for the hardships imposed by the Christian Church there was an approved Christian remedy. Thomas Aquinas, the greatest authority on morals in Europe in the thirteenth century, had written : " If rulers think they harm their souls by taking money from usurers, let them remember that they are themselves to blame. They ought to see that the Jews are compelled to labour as they do in some parts of Italy."[1] A Christian king, and one whom Edward revered as his old leader in arms and as a model of piety, had already acted in accordance with the teaching of Thomas Aquinas. In 1253 St. Louis sent from the Holy Land an order that all Jews should leave France for ever, except those who should become traders and workers with their hands.[2] And now, when Edward was forbidding the Jews of England to practise usury, he naturally dealt with them in the fashion recommended by the great teacher of his time and adopted by the saintly king " The King also grants," said the Statute of 1275, " that the Jews may practise merchandise, or live by their labour, and for those purposes freely converse with Christians. Excepting that, upon any pretence whatever, they shall not be levant or couchant amongst them ; nor on account of their merchandise be in scots, lots, or talliage with the other inhabitants of those cities or boroughs where they remain ; seeing they are talliable to the King as his own serfs, and not otherwise. . . . And further the King grants, that such as are unskilful in merchandise, and cannot labour, may take lands to farm, for any term not exceeding ten years, provided no homage, fealty, or any such kind of service, or advowson to Holy Church, be belonging to them. Provided also that this power to farm

---

[1] Thomas Aquinas, *Opusculum*, XXI. (*Ad Ducissam Brabantiae* in Vol. XIX. of the Venice edition, 1775-88.)

[2] M. Paris, *Chronica Majora*, V. 361, 2.

lands, shall continue in force for ten years from the making
of this Act, and no longer." [1]

The 16,000[2] Jews of England were thus called upon
to change at once their old occupation for a new one, and
the task was imposed upon them under conditions which
made it all but impossible of fulfilment. They were
forbidden to become burgesses of towns ; and the effect of
the prohibition was to make it impossible for them, in most
parts of England, to become traders, for it practically excluded them from the Gild Merchant. It is true that some
towns professed that their Gild was open to all the
inhabitants, whether burgesses or not, so long as they took
the oath to preserve the liberties of the town and the king's
peace.[3] But most of the Gilds were exclusive bodies, to
which all non-burgesses would find it hard to gain
admission,[4] and Jewish non-burgesses, though not as a
rule kept out by a disqualifying religious formula,[5] would
on account of the unpopularity of their race and religion,
find it trebly hard.[6] As non-Gildsmen, they would be at
a disadvantage both in buying goods and in selling them.
They would find it hard to buy, because, in some towns at
any rate, the Gildsmen were accustomed to " oppress the
people coming to the town with vendible wares, so that no
man could sell his wares to anyone except to a member of
the society." [7] They would find it in all towns hard to sell,
in some impossible. In some towns non-Gildsmen were
forbidden to deal in certain articles of common use,

---

[1] Blunt, *Establishment and Residence,* etc., 141.
[2] This is the number of those who left the country in 1290. *Flores*
Historiarum (Rolls Series), iii. 70. Probably the number of those in the
country in 1275 was about the same.
[3] Gross, *The Gild Merchant,* I. 38.   [4] *Ibid.,* I. 39-40.
[5] *Ibid.* II., 68, 138, 214, 243. 257.
[6] One Jew alone is known to have become a member of a Gild during
the residence of the Jews in England before 1290. He became a citizen
at the same time. His election took place in 1263 (Kitchin's *Winchester—*
Historic Towns Series, p. 108), After 1275 it would have been illegal.
[7] Gross, *The Gild Merchant,* I. 41.

such as wool, hides, grain, untanned leather, and unfulled cloth ; in others, as in Southampton, they might not buy anything in the town to sell again there, or keep a wine tavern, or sell cloth by retail except on market day and fair day, or keep more than five quarters of corn in a granary to sell by retail. There were even towns where the municipal statutes altogether forbade non-Gildsmen to keep shops or to sell by retail.[1]

It was almost as difficult for Jews to become agriculturists or artisans, as to become traders. They were allowed by the statute to farm land, but for ten years only, and they were far too ignorant of agriculture to be able to take advantage of the permission. They could not work on the land of others as villeins, because, even if a Christian lord had been willing to receive them, they would have been prevented by their religion from taking the oath of fealty.[2]

Only under exceptional conditions could they work at handicrafts. A Jew who possessed manual dexterity might, as was sometimes done in the thirteenth century, have worked for himself at a cottage industry, and might, though the task would have been a hard one, have gained a connection among Christians, and induced them to trust him with materials.[3] But many crafts were at the time coming under the regulations of craft-gilds. Certainly as early as the beginning of the fourteenth century, there were in London fully-organised gilds of Lorimers, Weavers, Tapicers, Cap-makers, Saddlers, Joiners, Girdlers, and Cutlers.[4] In Hereford there were Gilds for nearly thirty trades.[5] It was probably very often the case, as it was with the Weavers' Gild in London, that a craft-gild existing

[1] Gross, *The Gild Merchant*, I. 45, 46, 47.

[2] *Liber Custumarum* (Rolls Series), 215.

[3] Ochenkowski, *Englands Wirthschaftliche Entwickelung im Ausgange des Mittelalters*, 51-4.

[4] *Liber Custumarum* (Rolls Series) 80-81, 101-2, 121 ; *Liber Albus* (Rolls Series), 726, 734.   Riley, *Memorials of London*, 179.

[5] Johnson, *Customs of Hereford*, 115-6.

in any town could forbid the practice of the craft in the
town to all who had not been elected to membership, or
earned it by serving the apprenticeship that the Gild's
statute required.[1] The period required by the Lorimers'
statute was ten years, by the Weavers', seven, and in some
cases certainly, and probably in all, the apprenticeship had
to be served under a freeman of the city.[2] The apprentice
who had served his time, was still, in some towns and
industries, unable to practise his craft, unless he became a
citizen and entered the frank pledge.[3] It was difficult for
a Jewish boy to become an apprentice, since the Church
threatened to excommunicate any Christian who received
into his house, as an apprentice would naturally be received,
a Jew or Jewess; it was impossible for a Jewish man to
become a citizen, for the king forbade his Jewish " serfs "
to be in scot and lot with the other inhabitants of the cities
in which they lived.

Excluded from the trades and handicrafts of the towns,
the Jew might try other means of earning a livelihood.
He might attempt to travel with wares or with produce,
from one part of England to another, or he might be an
importer or an exporter. But wholesale trade of this kind
would be open to those alone who had command of a large
capital. And this was not the only difficulty in the way.
If the Jew went about the country with his goods from
fair to fair, or from city to city, he would do so at very
great risk. He would have to travel over the high roads,
the perils of which made necessary the Statute of Winchester, and are recounted in the words of its preamble,
*de jour en jour roberies, homicides, arsons, plus sovencrement
sont fetes que avaunt ne soleyent.*[4] If he survived the
dangers of the road and reached a fair, he would find

---

[1] *Liber Custumarum*, 418-425.

[2] *Liber Custumarum*, 78, 81, 124. Riley, *Memorials of London*, 179,
216.

[3] *Liber Custumarum*, 79. Ochenkowski, *Op. Cit.*, 64.

[4] Stubbs, *Select Charters*, 470.

there an assemblage made up in part of "daring persons," such as those, who, in spite of the orderly traders and citizens, had caused the massacre at Lynn in 1190,[1] or those who at Boston killed the merchants and plundered their goods, until "the streets ran with silver and gold,"[2] or those citizens of Winchester who, in the reign of Henry III., carried on for a time a successful conspiracy to rob all itinerant merchants who passed through the country.[3] With his foreign face and striking badge, he would be the first mark for the hatred of the riotous crowd. And if he escaped violence and robbery, he had still to fear the officials of the lord of the fair, who exercised for the time unlimited and irresponsible power, and who, according to the regulations of some fairs, could destroy the goods of any trader if their quality did not please them.[4] When he had managed to escape from the mob and the officials, his difficulties were not over. He might make his bargains, but there was no court of justice to which he could appeal to enforce the completion of any transaction that required a longer time than that of the duration of the fair. Redress for any injustice committed at a fair, or for the failure to carry out an agreement made there, could be obtained only through application made by the municipality of the complainant to that of the wrong-doer.[5] The Jew had no municipality to present his claims. If those with whom he had transactions deceived him, or refused to pay him, he was helpless. There was no power to which he could appeal.

If instead of going to a fair he tried to sell, in a town, produce from another country or from a different part of England, he was in a position of even greater difficulty.

---

[1] Jacobs, 116.

[2] Walsingham, *Historia Anglicana* (Rolls Series), I. 30.

[3] M. Paris, *Chronica Majora*, v. 56-8.

[4] Ochenkowski, *Englands wirthschaftliche Entwickelung*, 157.

[5] Cunningham, *Growth of English Industry and Commerce, Early and Middle Ages*, 175.

In a strange town he was as much an alien as in a strange
country, and there was scarcely any limit to the vexations
and sufferings that on that account he would have to endure.
In London, for example, alien merchants were forbidden to
remain in the city for more than forty consecutive days.
While they were there they might not sell anything by retail,
nor have any business dealings at all with any but citizens.
There was a long list of articles that they were altogether
forbidden to buy. They might not stow their goods in
houses or cellars; they had to sell within forty days all
that they had brought with them; they were allowed
neither to sell anything after that time, nor to take
anything back with them. They were continually annoyed
by the officers of the city.[1] All these disadvantages the
Jew would have to endure to the full while competing with
many powerful organisations which were engaged in foreign
trade, and had, after long struggles, secured from the king
special charters of privilege. Such were the companies
of the merchants of Germany, who had their steelyard in
London and their settlements at Boston and Lynn; the
Flemings, who had their Hanse in London; the Gascons
who enjoyed a charter; the Spaniards and Portuguese; the
Florentines, most powerful of all, and the Venetians,
whose enterprise was, at the beginning of the fourteenth
century at any rate, carried on under the auspices of the
Republic.[2]

The last opportunity for the Jews was to take part in
the export of English produce. English wool was the
most important article of international trade in Western
Europe. It was brought from monasteries and landholders
chiefly by the rich and powerful companies of Flemish

---

[1] *Liber Custumarum* (Rolls Series), xxxiv.-xlviii., 61-72; *Liber Albus*,
xcv., xcvi., 287; Macpherson, *Annals of Commerce*, I. 388-9.

[2] *Liber Custumarum* and *Liber Albus*, as referred to in preceding note:
Cunningham, *Growth of English Industry and Commerce, Early and
Middle Ages*, 181-6; Ochenkowski, *Englands wirthschaftliche Entwickelung*, 180; *Calendar of State Papers (Venetian)*, lx.-lxix.; Peruzzi, *Storia
dei Banchieri e del Commercio di Firenze*, 70.

and Italian merchants, and sent to Flanders and Italy to be woven and dyed.[1] The Jews had, apparently, long taken some slight part in wholesale trade,[2] but the amount of capital that it required, and the power of the rivals who held the field, made it impossible for many of them to take to it immediately as a substitute for money-lending. Still it was the only form of enterprise in which they would not be at a hopeless disadvantage : and some Jews, those probably who had a large capital and were able to recall it from the borrowers, followed the example of the Italians, and made to landholders advances of money to be repaid in corn and wool.[3]

VIII.—THE TEMPTATIONS OF THE JEWS.

But even for those Jews who were rich enough to take part in wholesale trade, there was still a great temptation to transgress the prohibition against usury. All the legal machinery that was necessary for the due execution and validity of agreements between Jews and Christians—the chest in which the deeds were deposited, and the staffs of officers by whom they were registered and supervised —were still maintained in some towns, since they were necessary alike for the recovery, by the ordinary process, of the old debts (many of which, in spite of the order for summary repayment in the Statute of 1275, still remained outstanding)[4] and for the registration of any new agree-

---

[1] Cunningham, *Growth*, etc., 185 ; Macpherson. *Annals of Commerce* pp. 115, 481 : *Calendar of State Papers* (*Venetian*), lxvi.-lxvii.

[2] Jacobs, 66-7 ; *Archæological Journal*, xxxviii. 179.

[3] This was the procedure adopted by the Italians :   They paid down a sum as earnest-money, and then took a bond (Peruzzi, 70). Cf. Tovey, 207.

[4] For pledges still unredeemed, land still in the hands of the Jews and old debts still unpaid long after the Statutes of 1270-1275 had been passed, see MSS. in Public Record Office (*Queen's Remembrancer's Miscellanea*, 557, 13-23) ; Rymer, I. 570; John of Peckham, I. 937; *Calendar of Patent Rolls*, 1281-1292, p. 81 ; Prynne, *Second Demurrer*, pp. 74 and 80 (=154).

ments that might be made for the delivery of corn and
wool, or for the repayment of money lent ostensibly
without interest. There was no lack of would-be borrowers to co-operate with the Jews in using this machinery
in order to make agreements on which, in spite of the
prohibition of usury, money might profitably be lent. The
demand for loans was great, far too great to be satisfied,
as the Church thought it reasonable to expect,[1] by money
advanced without interest; and owing to the progress of
the change from payment of rents in kind or service to
payment in cash,[2] it was steadily growing. It had been
met by the money of the Italian bankers, of the Jews, of
English citizens, and, as is freely hinted by writers of the
time, of great English barons, who secretly shared in the
transactions and the profits of the Jewish and foreign
usurers.[3] The supply had suddenly been checked by the
simultaneous prohibition of all usury whether of Jews or of
Christians. Now a Jew who wished, by collusion with a
borrower, to evade the law against usury, had only to study
the methods that had been followed by the Caursines, and
those that were still followed by the Italians and acquiesced
in by the heads of the religious houses with whom they
had dealings. The Caursines, for example, sometimes
avoided the appearance of usury by lending 100 marks
and receiving in return a bond, acknowledging a loan of
£100.[4] Sometimes they lent money for a definite period,
on an agreement that they were to get a "gift," in return
for their kindness in making the loan, and "compensation"
in case it were not repaid in time.[5] Sometimes by a still
more elaborate device, the Italians combined their two

---

[1] Labbeus, *Sacrosancta Concilia*, XI. 649-50.

[2] Vinogradoff, *Villeinage in England*, 179, 307.

[3] M. Paris, V. 245; Wilkins, *Conc.*, I. 675; *De Antiq. Legibus*, 234 sq.
(Archbishop of York's remarks on the corruption of the Great Council and
on the *fautores* of Jews.)

[4] M. Paris, *Chronica Majora*, V. 404-5.

[5] Muratori, *Antiquitates Italicæ Medii Aevi*. I., 893.

professions of money-lenders and merchants, by inducing
a monastery which had borrowed money, to acknowledge
the receipt, not only of the sum actually received, but also
of the price of certain sacks of wool which it bound itself
in due time to supply.[1]   The Jews, no doubt, followed the
example of the Caursines and of the Italians.   In official
registers, which are still extant, there are mentioned bonds
which secured to Jewish creditors a large payment in money
together with a small payment in kind, and which doubtless represent collusive transactions, in which the offence of
usury was to be avoided by the substitution of a recompense in kind for interest in money.   Other bonds for
repayment of money alone are mentioned in the same
registers as having been executed after 1275, and every one
of the kind that was executed between that date and the
date of the amendment of the Statute against usury may
be safely considered to represent a transaction which was
an offence, either veiled or open, against the prohibition.[2]

The temptation to transgress the Statute of 1275 could
appeal only to Jews with capital, but on the poorer Jews
other temptations acted with even more strength and even
worse results.

The only reputable careers known to have been
open to the poorer Jews were to become servants in the
houses of their rich co-religionists,[3] or else to imitate in a
humble way their financial transactions, either by keeping
pawnshops,[4] or by carrying on, in towns where there was
no recognised Jewry, business of the same kind as that
of the rich money-lenders in the larger Jewish settlements.
To follow these pursuits was now impossible, in consequence,
not only of the prohibition of usury, but also of the strict-
ness with which Edward enforced the old legislation

[1] *Rotuli Parliamentorum*, I. 1, 2.
[2] "The Debts and Houses of the Jews of Hereford," in *Transactions of
the Jewish Historical Society of England*, vol. 1.
[3] *Royal Letters* (Rolls Series), II. 21.
[4] *Leet Jurisdiction of Norwich* (Selden Society), p. 10; Cf. *Ancren
Riwle* (Camden Society), 395. "Do not men account him a good friend
who layeth his pledge in *Jewry* to redeem his companion?"

against the residence of Jews in towns where there did no
exist a chest for the deposit of Jewish debts, and a staff of
clerks to witness and register them.[1] There was thus
nothing to which the poorer Jews could turn. Crowded
as unwelcome intruders into a small and decreasing number
of towns,[2] without legal standing or industrial skill, hated
by the people and declared accursed by the Church, they
were bidden to support themselves under conditions which
made the task impossible unless they could take by storm
the citadel of municipal privilege which bade defiance to
the "greatest of the Plantagenets" throughout his reign.

Under such conditions degeneration was inevitable. Some
of the Jews are said to have taken to highway robbery
and burglary;[3] some went into the House of Converts,
where they got 1½d. a day and free lodging.[4] But to the
dishonest there was open a far more profitable form of
dishonesty than either of those already mentioned, viz.,
clipping the coin.

The offence had long been prevalent. In 1248 such
mischief had been done that, according to Matthew Paris
"no foreigner, let alone an Englishman, could look on an
English coin with dry eyes and unbroken heart."[5] It was
in vain that Henry III. issued a new coinage, so stamped
that the device and the lettering extended to the edge of
the piece,[6] and caused it to be proclaimed in every town,
village, market-place, and fair that none but the new pieces
with their shapes unaltered should be given or taken in
exchange.[7] The opportunity for dishonesty was too tempting. The coins that actually circulated in the country

[1] Rymer, *Foedera*, I. 503, 634; *Papers of the Anglo-Jewish Historical Exhibition*, 187-190.
[2] *Norfolk Antiquarian Miscellany*, I. 326, quoted *supra*, p. 20 (*n*. 3).
[3] *Calendar of Patent Rolls*, 1281-1292, p. 93; *Papers Anglo-Jewish Hist. Ex.* 167.
[4] See *Dictionary of Political Economy*, Article JEWS, (House for Converted).
[5] *Chronica Majora*, V. 15.
[6] *Annales Monastici* (Rolls Series), II. 339.
[7] M. Paris, *Chronica Majora*, V. 15, 16.

were of many different issues,[1] they were not milled at the
edges,[2] they were so liable to damage and mutilation of all
kinds that their deficiency of weight had to be recognised
and allowed for.[3] Hence anyone who had many coins
passing through his hands could secure an easy profit by
clipping off a piece from each one before he passed it
again into circulation. In the early part of the reign of
Edward I., such was the deficiency in the weight of genuine
coins (an annalist of the period estimates it at 50 per cent.),[4]
and such the amount of false coin in circulation, that the
price of commodities rose to an alarming height, foreign
merchants were driven away, trade became completely dis-
organised, shopkeepers refused the money tendered to them,
and the necessities of life were withdrawn from the mar-
kets.[5] The King had to promise to issue a new coinage,
but the announcement of his intention only increased the
general disturbance. The Archbishop of Canterbury complained that in consequence of the disturbance of circulation,
he could not find anyone, except the professional usurers,
from whom he could borrow money on which to live during
the interval before the revenues of his see began to come
in.[6] When the King at this period of his reign went to
a priory to ask for money, the first and most cogent of the
excuses that he heard was that "the House was im-
poverished by the change in the coinage of the realm."[7]
Public opinion ascribed to the Jews the greatest share in
the injuries to the coinage. "They are notoriously forgers
and clippers of the coin," says Matthew Paris[8] And that
the suspicion was not absolutely without justification is
shown by the fact, that early in Henry III.'s reign, the

[1] Ruding, *Annals of the Coinage*, I. 179.
[2] Ashley. *Economic Hist., Theory*, I. 169.
[3] Ashley, I., 215, n. 95 ; cf. Jacobs. 73 and 225.
[4] *Annales Monastici* (Rolls Series), IV. 278.
[5] *Annales Monastici*, IV. 278 ; *Liber Custumarum*, 189.
[6] John of Peckham, *Registrum Epistolarum* (Rolls Series), I. 22.
[7] *Annales Monastici*, III. 295.   [8] *Historia Anglorum*, III. 76.

community made a payment to the King in order to secure as a concession the expulsion from England of such of its members as might be convicted of the crime.[1] When inquiries were ordered into the causes of the debasement, in 1248, it was generally considered that the guilt would be found to rest with the Jews.[2] The official verdict included them with the Caursines and the Flemish wool-merchants in its condemnation.[3]

It was not unnatural that Edward, when the evil reappeared in his reign, should share the general suspicion against the Jews, seeing that they had only recently begun to give up dealing in money, while many of the poorer among them must have become, since 1275, desperate enough to be ready to take to any tempting form of dishonesty. The King's indignation at the suffering that had been caused by the injury done to the old coinage, and at the expense that was involved in the preparation of the new issue which had become necessary, prompted him to act on his suspicions, and to take a measure of terrible severity in order to make sure of the apprehension of the most probable culprits. When, in 1278, he was making preparations for an inquiry into the whole subject of the coinage, he caused all the Jews of England to be imprisoned in one night, their property to be seized, and their houses to be searched. At the same time the goldsmiths, and many others against whom information was given by the Jews, were treated in the same way.[4]

The prisoners were tried before a bench of judges and royal officers. There can be no doubt that many innocent men were accused, even if they were not condemned At a time when all the Jews in England were imprisoned, there was a great temptation for Christians to bring false

---

[1] Tovey, 109 ; Madox, *History of the Exchequer* I. 245, z.

[2] M. Paris, *Chronica Majora*, IV. 608.

[3] *Ibid.*, V. 16.

[4] *Annales Monastici*, IV. 278.

accusations against those among them whom they dis-
liked on personal or religious grounds, especially as there
was a good chance of extorting hush-money from the
accused, or, in case of condemnation, of concealing from
the escheators some of their property.[1] The Jews and the
King recognised the danger One Manser of London, for example, was wise enough to sue that an investigation might
be held into the ownership of tools for clipping that were
found on the roof of his house.[2] The King, anxious that
punishment should fall only on the guilty, issued a general
writ, in which the various motives for false accusation were
recited, and it was ordered that any Jew against whom no
charge had been brought by a certain date might secure
himself altogether by paying a fine.[3] Nevertheless, a large
number both of Jews and Christians were found guilty. Of
the Christians only three were condemned to death, though
many others were heavily fined. For the Jews, however,
there was no mercy. Two hundred and ninety-three of
them were hanged and drawn in London, and all their
property escheated to the King. A few more had been
condemned, but saved their lives by conversion to
Christianity.[4]

The activity with which Jews took part, or were supposed
to take part, in the debasement of the coinage, and in the prohibited practice of usury,[5] must have aroused in the mind of

---

[1] *Calendar of Patent Rolls from* 1281 *to* 1292, 128, 147, 173, 176, 213,
201, 451 ; *Chron. Ed. I.*, I. 93 ; *Rotuli Parliamentorum*, I. 51a ; Rymer,
Fædera, I., 570.

[2] *Papers Anglo-Jewish Historical Exhibition*, 42-3.

[3] Tovey, 211-13.

[4] *Chronicles of Edward I. and Edward II.* (Rolls Series), I., 88 ;
Chronicon Petroburgense (Camden Society), 29.

[5] " Whereas in the time of our ancestors, kings of England,
loans at interest were wont and were allowed to be made by Jews
of our kingdom, and much of such profits fell into the hands of
those our ancestors, as the issues of our Jewry ; and we, led on
by the love of God, and wishing to follow more devoutly in the

the King some misgivings on the subject of his new policy.
Nevertheless, he did not as yet despair of its ultimate
success. The crimes of the Jews were no greater than
those of the Christians around them, though they called
forth heavier punishment. Christians clipped and coined ;
Christians still lent money on usury.[1] And a certain
amount of crime among Jews could not but be looked for
as a natural result of the terrible difficulties in the way of
the social revolution that had been demanded of them.
Edward saw that he had been trying to do too much at
once. The Jews could not change their occupation as
suddenly as he had wished. The country could not do
without money-lenders. By making the lending of money
at interest a penal offence, and thus encouraging debtors
and creditors to keep their transactions secret, Edward had
weakened the supervision that had been exercised by the
Treasury, since 1194, over the business and property of
the Jews, and thus he had increased the chance of fraud in
the collection of tallages, and in the apportionment of the
share of each estate that had long been claimed by the

---

path of the Holy Church, did forbid unto all the Jews of our
kingdom who had viciously lived from such loans, that none of them
henceforth in any manner be guilty of resorting to loans at interest,
but that they seek their living and sustain themselves by other legitimate
work and merchandise, especially since by the favour of Holy Church
they are suffered to sell and live among Christians. Nevertheless,
afterwards, in a blind and evil spirit, turning to evil, under colour of
merchandise and good contracts and covenants, what we established
by rational thought, premeditating mischief anew, they do it
with Christians by means of bonds and divers instruments, which
remain with the Jews, and in which, on a given debt or contract,
they put double, treble, or quadruple more than they lend to the
Christians [this reads like an exaggeration], penally abusing the name
of usury. . . ." (*Papers Anglo-Jewish Historical Exhibition*, 225-6).

[1] For Coining, see Ruding. *Annals of the Coinage* I. 197 ; *Calendar of
Patent Rolls from* 1281 *to* 1292, 97 ; *Abbreviatio Rotulorum Originalium*
(Record Commission), 49 ; Peckham. *Registrum Epistolarum*. I. 146. For
Usury, *Forty-fourth Report of the Deputy-Keeper of the Public Records*,
pp. 8 and 9 ; *Archæologia*, XXVIII., 227-9 ; Peckham, II., 542 ; and for a
later period. *Rotuli Parliamentorum*, II. 332a, (VII.) 350b.

Crown as the succession due on Jewish property.[1] But he had not stamped out usury, though the Statute of 1275 had forbidden it. He had not even secured the redemption of all pledges of Christians from the hands of the Jews, though the Statute of 1275 had demanded it. And, therefore, in order that he might not keep on the Statute Book a law of which the effective administration was impossible, he mitigated the severity of the provisions of 1275, and issued, probably a few years later, a new Statute, in which he prescribed certain conditions under which usury was to be permitted. He allowed loans to be made under contract for the payment of interest at the rate of half a mark in the pound yearly, but for three years only ; and, in order to reduce the temptation to conclude secret transactions, restored legal recognition to all debts of the value of £20 or upwards that were made under the prescribed conditions, and were registered before the chirographer and clerk, and threatened heavy penalties against all who should lend up to that amount without registration.[2]

Edward was wise in thus substituting for his earlier, harassing measure, one that allowed for gradual change, and that attempted to control the evil of which the immediate suppression was impossible. But the few years' experience that he had already had ought to have made him go farther still. It ought to have shown him that it was hopeless to expect the Jews to give up usury so long as the greater part of them were practically excluded from all other pursuits, and that, if ever he was to bring to a successful issue the policy that he had inaugurated, he would have to find some means of enabling them to work side by side with Christians, and to compete with them on equal conditions.

Such a task would have been full of difficulties, the

[1] *Papers of Anglo-Jewish Historical Exhibition,* p. 192 (note 54) and p. 222.

[2] *Papers of Anglo-Jewish Historical Exhibition,* pp. 224-9.

greatest of which resulted from the active hostility with
which the rulers and teachers of the Christian Church in
the thirteenth century, unlike their predecessors, regarded
the Jews. The growth and nature of this hostility must
now be considered.

IX.—The Jews in Relation to the Church of the Thirteenth Century.

The Popes of the earlier part of the Middle Ages had
found enough employment for their energies in the effort
to maintain their own position in Christendom; and they
had neither the wish nor the power to seek a conflict with
a race that remained wholly outside the Church. In the
twelfth century there was no other general Church Law
directed against the Jews than that which forbade them to
live in the same houses with Christians, and to have Christian servants.[1] In England especially, Churchmen of the
twelfth century showed towards the Jews a tolerant spirit,
and made no effort to augment their unpopularity or to
diminish their privileges. The examples of Anselm, and of
his contemporary, Gilbert of Westminster, show that in the
attempts made at that time by men of high position in the
Church to convert the Jews, no method was employed
except that of reasonable persuasion.[2] Churches and
monasteries took charge, at times of danger, of the money,
and even of the families, of Jews. Such friendly intercourse as existed between Jews and Christians was
allowed to go on without any attempt at ecclesiastical
interference.[3]

The accession of Innocent the Third to the pontificate

---

[1] See the Decrees of the Third Lateran Council of 1179, Mansi, *Concilia*,
XXII., 231.

[2] St. Anselm, *Epistolæ*, III., 117 (Migne, *Patrologiæ Cursus Completus*,
Vol. 159, columns 153-155); Gilbert of Westminster, *Disputatio Judaici
cum Christiano* (Ibid. 1005-1036).

[3] *Chronicles of Stephen, Henry II., and Richard I.* (Rolls Series), I.,

brought about a rapid change in the attitude of the
Church towards the Jews. Innocent was the first to advance, on behalf of the Papacy, the claim that the Lord
gave Peter not only the whole Church, but the whole
world to rule,[1] and he endeavoured with a merciless
enthusiasm, from which all unbelievers and heretics in
Christian countries had to suffer, to make good his claim,
and to establish in Europe one united Catholic Church.
He took his stand on the doctrine, which his predecessors
had held[2] in a modified form, and without ever acting on
it, that the Jews were condemned to perpetual slavery on
account of the wickedness of their ancestors in crucifying
Christ ; and he thought that they ought to be made to feel,
and their neighbours likewise, that it was only out of
Christian pity that their presence was endured in Christian
countries.

The position of the Jews at the time of Innocent's accession to the pontificate was very far from being such as his
theory required. They had magnificent synagogues, they
employed Christian servants, they married, or were said to
marry, Christian wives : they refused, in what some Christians regarded as a spirit of outrageous insolence, to eat
the same meat and to drink the same wine as the Gentiles,
and they made no secret of their disbelief in the sacred

---

310 (among the victims of the massacre at Lynn in 1190 was *quidam
Judæus, insignis medicus, qui et artis et modestiæ suæ gratia Christianis
quoque familiaris et honorabilis fuerat*) ; *Gervase of Canterbury* (Rolls
Series). I.. 405. (The Jews help the monks of Canterbury in their struggle
with the Archbishop in 1188) ; *Rotuli Litterarum Clausarum* (Record
Commission). I.. 20b. (*Rex, &c., domino Lincolniensi Episcopo, &c.;
mandamus vobis quod non permittatis injuste catalle Judæorum receptari
in ecclesiis in diœcesi vestra.* February 28th. 1205) ; *Chronica Jocelini de
Brakelonde* (Camden Society). p. 33. (A.D. 1190. *Abbas jussit solempniter
excommunicari illos qui de cetero receptarent Judeos vel in hospicio
reciperent in villa Sancti Edmundi*) ; Jacobs, *The Jews of Angevin
England*. 269. ("*English Jews drink with Gentiles*.")

[1] Moeller. *History of the Christian Church, Middle Ages* (Eng. Tr.).
p. 279.

[2] Mansi. *Concilia*. XXII. 231.

history of Christianity. Moreover, they were suspected of exercising a considerable influence on the growth of the heresies which it was the chief work of Innocent's life to combat. The Vaudois, the Cathari, and the Albigenses, all kept up Jewish observances, and were said to have learnt from the Jews their heretical dogmas ; the Albigenses, indeed, were accused of maintaining that the law of the Jews was better than the law of the Christians. And, nevertheless, Christian kings supported the Jews in every way. They countenanced their usury, they refused (so, at least, Innocent said) to allow evidence against them on any charge to be given by Christian witnesses, and they even employed them in high offices of State. In view of these facts, Innocent thought that a great effort of repression should be made, and he wrote to the King of France, the Duke of Burgundy, and other monarchs, asking for their assistance in the work of reducing the Jews to that condition of slavery which was their due. He decreed in his general Church Council that Jews should be excluded in future from public offices, and that they should wear a badge to distinguish them from Christians; and he renewed the old regulation of the Church, which required them to dismiss Christian servants from their houses. In order to ensure that the last provision should be observed, he decided that any Christians having any intercourse with Jews that transgressed it should be subject to excommunication. For the enforcement of his other anti-Jewish measures he relied on the help of the temporal power in all Christian countries.[1]

The declaration of war made by Innocent III. was a terrible calamity for the Jews: but though it affected at

---

[1] Letters of Innocent (Migne. *Patrologiæ Cursus Completus*, Vols. 214-217) ; Lib. VII.. 186 ; Lib. VIII.. 50. 121 ; Lib. X.. 61. 190 ; *Corpus Juris Canonici* (Leipzig. 1839). II.. 747-8 ; Graetz. *Geschichte der Juden*. VII., 7. 8 ; Depping, *Les Juifs dans le Moyen Age*. 183 ; Hahn. *Geschichte der Ketzer*. III.. 6. 7 ; Hurter. *Geschichte Papst Innocenz der Dritten*. II.. 234 ; Gűdemann. *Geschichte des Erziehungswesens*. u.s.c.. I.. 37 ; Rule. *History of the Inquisition*. I. 10. 17.

once the whole of Christian Europe, still its evil results might have passed away in time. Popes were but men and politicians: and just as Innocent had, by the publication of his wishes and decrees concerning the Jews, set himself in opposition to his predecessors, so might his successors, in their turn, moved by different feelings or taking a different view of the interests and duties of the Church, set themselves in opposition to him, and go back to the old lenient opinions and practice. But within a few years of the death of Innocent, the work of attacking the Jews ceased to be in the hands of any one man, and passed over to a body of men habitually influenced not by personal or political considerations, but only by what they conceived to be the interest of religion, and filled with a hatred of the Jews more fierce and fanatical and steadfast than that of the Popes could ever have been.

The Dominican order was formally constituted in 1223, and from the earliest years of its existence devoted itself to the task of rooting out unbelief from the Christian world. The work that its members at first professed to regard as peculiarly their own was that of preaching, but on the Jews their preaching had no effect. With an ingenuity and determination worthy of the order that in a later century was to provide the Inquisition with its chief ministers, the Dominicans devised and carried out another plan of action. Assisted by converted Jews who had joined them, they undertook the study of Hebrew, and their master, Raymundus de Peñaforte, induced the King of Spain to build and endow seminaries for the purpose.[1] Armed with this new knowledge, they were able to attack first, what they represented as the foolish and pernicious contents of such Jewish books as the Talmud, and secondly, the stubbornness of the Jews who refused to accept the doctrines of Christianity, the truth of which the Dominicans professed to be able to demonstrate from the Old Testament. Two incidents which must at the

---

[1] Graetz. *Geschichte der Juden.* VII., 27.

time have been famous throughout Europe illustrate their method of warfare. In 1239 Nicolas Donin, a converted Jew who had become a Dominican friar, laid before Gregory IX. a series of statements concerning the Talmud. Helped, no doubt, by all the influence of his order, he induced the Pope to issue bulls to the Kings of France, England, and Spain, and the bishops in those countries, ordering that all copies of the Talmud should be seized, and that public inquiry should be held concerning the charges brought against the book. In England and Spain nothing seems to have been done, but in Paris the Pope's instructions were carried out, and, at the instigation of the leading Dominicans, St. Louis ordered that all copies of the Talmud that could be found in France should be confiscated, and that four Rabbis should, on behalf of the Jews, hold a public debate with Donin, in order to meet, if they could, the charges that he was prepared to maintain. In the course of the debate, which was held in the precincts of the Court and in the presence of members of the Royal family and great dignitaries of the Church, Donin asserted that the Talmud encouraged the Jews to despise, deceive, rob, and even murder Christians, that it contained blasphemous falsehoods concerning Christ, superstitions and puerilities of all kinds, and passages disrespectful to God and inconsistent with morality. The Rabbis answered as best they could, but the court of Inquisitors decided that the charges had been substantiated, and ordered that all the confiscated copies of the Talmud should be burnt. After a delay of about two years the *Auto-da-fe* took place, and fourteen cartloads of the Talmud were sacrificed.[1] The other famous incident of the kind took place in Spain. Pablo Christiano, a converted Jew, who, like Donin, had joined the Dominicans, challenged the Jews of Aragon to a discussion on the differences between Judaism and Chris-

---

[1] *Revue des Etudes Juives*, I. 247, 293 ; II. 248 ; III. 39 ; Noel Valois, *Guillaume d'Auvergne*, pp. 118, 137.

tianity, and induced James I. to compel them to take
up the challenge. The famous Nachmanides came forward as the representative of his co-religionists. Pablo
undertook to show that the Old Testament, and other
books recognised by the Jews, taught that the Messiah
had come, that he was "very God and very man,"
that he suffered and died for the salvation of mankind,
and that with his advent the ceremonial law ceased to
be of any effect. Nachmanides denied that any of these
propositions could be substantiated from the Jewish
sacred books. For four days the disputation was carried
on in the presence of the king and many great personages
of Church and State. Of course the verdict was that the
Christian disputant had beaten the Jew.[1]

The method of conducting these two controversies showed
that the Dominicans were determined to use every possible
weapon against the Jews. The Talmud, a huge, heterogeneous and unedited compilation, contains passages
which are trivial and foolish, and others, written by men
who had memories of persecution fresh in their minds,
which express bitter hatred towards the "Gentiles," that is,
the Romans who had taken Jerusalem, and had destroyed
the nationality of the Jewish race. It was easy for an
opponent to pick out such passages, to assert that what
was said against the "Gentiles" expressed, not the feelings
of the victims of persecution against the Romans of the
second century, but the feelings of all Jews towards all
non-Jews, at every time and at every place, and to convince
an uncritical audience that those who held in honour the
book that contained such passages were enemies of religion,
against whose influence it behoved all Christian powers to
guard the faithful. Similarly, by compelling the Jews to
take part in a discussion concerning the prophecies of the
Old Testament, the Dominicans imposed on them the choice
between the two alternatives of betraying their religion by

---

[1] *Histoire Littéraire de la France,* XXVII., 562-3 ; Graetz, *Geschichte,*
VII., 131, 135.

acquiescing in what they believed to be a false interpreta-
tion of their scripture, or else of proclaiming publicly their
disbelief in doctrines which were at the very foundation
of Christianity. The effect on the ruling classes in Europe
of the two discussions just mentioned must have been very
great. And the Dominicans were continually carrying on
the same work, though, of course, seldom before audiences
so distinguished. Pablo, for example, travelled about Spain
and Provence, compelling the Jews, by virtue of a royal
edict that had been issued in his favour, to hold disputes
with him on matters of religion.[1] Many other members of
the order devoted their lives to the same pursuit,[2] and thus
did their best to fill the rulers of the Church with a dread
of the terrible consequences that the existence of Judaism
threatened to the Christian religion.

And, unfortunately for the Jews, their religion began to
be feared at the same time as cruel and powerful fanatics
like Innocent and the Dominicans were doing their best to
cause it to be hated. There is good reason to believe,
though detailed evidence is not abundant, that towards the
end of the Middle Ages Judaism exercised over the superstitions of other faiths the same fascination as in the first
century of the Roman Empire. Thomas Aquinas believed
that unrestricted intercourse between Jews and Christians
was likely to result in the conversion of Christians to
Judaism, and for that reason he thought it right, in spite
of the general liberality of his opinions concerning the
Jews, that intercourse with them should be allowed to such
Christians alone as were strong in the faith, and were more
likely to convert them than to be converted by them.[3] "It
happens sometimes," wrote a Pope of the thirteenth century, "that Christians, when they are visited by the Lord
with sickness and tribulation, go astray, and have recourse

---

[1] Graetz, *Geschichte der Juden*, VII., 135 ; J. Jacobs, *Inquiry into the
Sources of the History of the Jews in Spain*, xviii., 18.

[2] *Scriptores Ordinis Prædicatorum* (Quétif and Echard), I., 246, 396,
398, 594.

[3] Thomas Aquinas, *Summa Theologiæ*, Secunda Secundæ, Quæstio X.

to the vain help of the Jewish rite. They hold in the synagogues of the Jews torches and lighted candles, and make offerings there. Likewise they keep vigils (especially on the Sabbath), in the hope that the sick may be restored to health, that those at sea may reach harbour, that those in childbirth may be safely delivered, and that the barren may become fruitful and rejoice in offspring. For the accomplishment of these and other wishes, they implore the help of the said rite, and in idolatrous fashion show open signs of devotion and reverence to a scroll, not without much harm to the orthodox faith, contumely to our Creator, and opprobrium and shame to the Universal Church."[1]

The anti-Jewish feeling that grew up from the causes that have just been described called into existence new institutions and measures designed for the purpose of humbling the Jews and checking the growth of Judaism. In compliance with the cruel request of Innocent, most of the monarchs of Europe compelled their Jewish subjects to wear a badge.[2] Local church councils, which hitherto had contented themselves with the attempt to enforce the old prohibition against the employment by Jews of Christian servants and nurses, now went further, and forbade Christians to allow the presence of Jews in their houses and taverns, to feast or dance with them, to be present at the celebration of their marriages, their new moons, and their festivals, and to employ their services as doctors.[3] The Popes of the latter part of the thirteenth century appointed Dominicans in various countries of Europe to perform the duty of preaching to the Jews, and of holding inquisitions into their heresies, in the hope that with the help of the secular power they might stamp them out.[4] In England the relation of the Jews to the Christians underwent somewhat the same changes as in Continental

---

[1] Baronius, *Annales Ecclesiastici* (ed. Theiner), XIII., 87.

[2] *Revue des Etudes Juives*, VI. 81 ; VII. 91.

[3] Mansi, *Concilia*, XXIII., 1171-6 ; Martène, *Thesaurus*, IV., 769.

[4] Depping, 198 ; Hahn, *Geschichte der Ketzer*, III., 13 ; Rule, *History of the Inquisition*, 27, 80, 81, 91, 332, 335-6.

Europe. Before the thirteenth century the Jews in England had, as has been said above, been free from molestation by the Church,[1] and their chief danger had been from the brutality and greed of the disorderly populace, of desperate outcasts, and of marauding Crusaders.[2] The first great attack made on them by any constituted power came from Stephen Langton, who, not content with passing at his Provincial Synod a decree which, in accordance with the regulations of Innocent, enforced the use of the badge and prohibited the erection of new synagogues, went so far as to issue orders that no one in his diocese should presume, under pain of excommunication, to have any intercourse with Jews, or should sell them any of the necessaries of life. The Bishops of Lincoln and Norwich issued the same orders in their dioceses.[3] Many other bishops in the reign of Henry III. did their best, partly by legislation in their diocesan synods and partly by the use of their personal and spiritual influence, to check intercourse between Jews and Christians.[4] Of course the king's guardians, in the interest of the royal income, a considerable part of which was derived from the Jewry, interfered to prevent the measures of Langton and his colleagues from being carried into effect. And Henry, when he took into his own hands the work of government, while, on the one hand, he showed his sympathy with the fears of the Church by building a house for the reception of Jewish converts,[5] and by lending the sanction of the civil power to the decree that ordered the use of the badge,[6] nevertheless followed the example that his guardians had set, and protected the Jews against the aggression of the Church.

[1] *Supra.* p. 53.   [2] *Supra*, pp. 12, 13, 19.
[3] Wilkins, *Magnæ Britanniæ Concilia.* I., 591 ; Tovey, *Anglia Judaica.* 83 ; Rye. *History of Norfolk*, 87.
[4] Wilkins, *Magnæ Britanniæ Concilia*, I., 657, 693, 719 ; *Letters of Bishop Grosseteste* (Rolls Series), 318.
[5] Matthew Paris, *Chronica Majora*, III., 262.
[6] Tovey. *Anglia Judaica*, 148.

There were many reasons which might have caused Edward to sympathise more strongly than his father had done, with the anti-Jewish feelings of the Church. He was a pious man and a pious king, filled with a sense of his kingly duty towards "the living God who takes to himself the souls of Princes."[1]   He was a Crusader, though the great crusading age was over, a founder of monasteries, a pilgrim to holy places; and through his confessors he was in close connection with, and under the influence of, the Dominican order.[2]   Some of his bishops were determined enemies of the Jews.   John of Peckham, for example, the Archbishop of Canterbury, insisted at one time on the demolition of all the small private synagogues in London, at which the Jews were in the habit of worshipping after the confiscation of their great public synagogues at the end of the reign of Henry III.; at another time he demanded from the king the help of the temporal power against Jews who having once been converted to Christianity, wished to go back to their old faith; on another occasion he took the bold step of writing to the Queen concerning her business transactions with the Jews, solemnly warning her that unless she gave them up she could never be absolved from her sins, "nay, not though an angel should assert the contrary."[3]   At Hereford, Bishop Swinfield was so determined to prevent intercourse with Jews that, when he heard that certain Christians intended to be present at a marriage feast to be given by some rich Jews of the city, he issued a proclamation threatening with excommunication any who should carry out their intention, and, when his proclamation was disregarded, he carried out his threat.[4]

[1] Rymer, *Fœdera*, I., 743.

[2] Tout, *Edward I.*, pp. 69, 149.

[3] John of Peckham, *Registrum Epistolarum* (Rolls Series), I., 239; II., 107; III., 937; Wilkins, *Magnæ Britanniæ Concilia*, II., 88-9; Prynne, *Second Demurrer*, 121-2.

[4] *Household Roll of Bishop Swinfield* (Camden Society), pp. c., ci.

Certain events that happened, or were said to have
happened, in England in Edward's lifetime, some, indeed,
under his own observation, may well have seemed to him
to justify the attitude of the Church. In 1275 a Dominican friar was converted to Judaism.[1] In 1268, while
Edward was in Oxford, the Chancellor, masters and
scholars of the University, and the Parochial Clergy, were
going in procession to visit the shrine of St. Friedswide
when, according to a story that gained general credence,
a Jew of the city snatched from the bearer a cross that
was being carried at their head and trod it under foot.[2]
At Norwich, early in Edward's reign, a Jew was burnt
for blasphemy.[3] At Nottingham, in 1278, a Jewess was
charged with abusing in scandalous terms all the Christian
bystanders in the market-place.[4]

Edward's conduct could not but be influenced by the
general tone of opinion in the Church, by the strong
anti-Jewish feeling of some of his bishops, and by the
follies, real or supposed, of the Jews themselves. In
continuation of his father's policy he made, throughout
his reign, such contributions as, with his scanty means, he
could afford, to the support of the House of Converts.[5] He
renewed the edict concerning the wearing of the badge,
and extended it to Jewesses, whereas it had formerly
applied only to Jews.[6] In order that the Dominicans
might be able to carry on in England the same efforts at
conversion as they were already pursuing in France, Spain
and Germany, he issued to all the sheriffs and bailiffs in
England writs bidding them do their best to induce all

[1] Graetz, *Geschichte der Juden.* VII., note 11. *Florence of Worcester*
(English Historical Society), II., 214.

[2] Tovey, *Anglia Judaica*, 168.

[3] *Forty-ninth Report of the Deputy-Keeper of the Public Records.*
p. 187.

[4] *Forty-seventh Report of the Deputy-Keeper of the Public Records.*
p. 306.

[5] *Dictionary of Political Economy.* Article. "Jews (House for Converted)."

[6] Tovey. *Anglia Judaica*, 208.

the Jews in the counties and towns under their charge
to assemble and hear the word of God preached by the
friars.[1] To meet the danger to religion that might arise
from the blasphemous utterances of Jews, he ordered that
proclamation should be made throughout England that
any Jew found guilty (after an enquiry conducted by
Christians) of having spoken disrespectfully of Christ, the
Virgin Mary, or the Catholic faith, should be liable to the
loss of life or limbs.[2]

Thus far, and no farther, was Edward prepared to go
with measures for the suppression of Judaism as a religion.
He believed that the Jews, so long as they remain Jews,
lived in ignorance and sin, and he did what he could to
help the friars in the effort to convert them. He believed
that some among them were likely to make blasphemous
attacks on Christianity, and he did what he could to keep
them in check. But he believed that it was possible for
them to live in peace and quietness, carrying on trades and
handicrafts, among Christian neighbours in Christian
towns. And it was to enable them to do so that he
adopted the policy of 1275, and bade the Jews renounce
usury, giving them at the same time permission "to practise trade, to live by their labour, and, for those purposes,
freely to converse with Christians." But, as we have seen,
there were imposed on the Jews who attempted to avail
themselves of this permission, legal disadvantages which
wholly unfitted them for industrial competition with non-
Jews, and compelled them to continue the practice of
usury. That Edward recognised this fact is shown by
the issue of the revised Statute of Usurers some years
after 1275; but that measure was inconclusive and inconsistent with the rest of his policy. Sooner or later the
conclusion would have forced itself on him that until the
Jews were, by the acquisition of the right to become
burgesses and gildsmen, enabled to enter into industrial

[1] *Forty-ninth Report of the Deputy-Keeper of the Public Records,*
p. 95 : Rymer, I., 576 ; Madox, *Exchequer,* I., 259.   [2] Tovey, p. 208.

competition on equal terms with Christians, all his efforts
to make them traders instead of usurers would be wasted.
He would then have had before him two alternatives. He
might, on the one hand, have declined to sacrifice his
seignorial rights over the Jews, whom he had described
in the Statute of 1275 as "talliable to the king as his own
serfs, and not otherwise," and in that case he would have
had to recognise that his whole Jewish policy was an
impossible one. Or he might, on the other hand, have
revoked the provision in the statute which forbade the
Jews to be in "scots, lots, or talliage with the other
inhabitants of those cities or burgesses where they remained." Such a measure would have been a step in the
only direction which could possibly lead to the success of
his policy. But it would not by itself have been enough
to secure success; for, when the legal difficulties of the
Jews had been removed, there would still have remained
the social difficulties which proceeded from the dislike in
which they were held by the Church and the people; and,
unless these difficulties also could be removed, so that the
Jews might be in a position of social equality, as well as
legal equality, with Christians, and associate with them
in friendly intercourse, the king's policy would be as far
from success as ever. Which alternative Edward would
have decided to adopt is, of course, a question we have
no means of answering; but the decision was taken out
of his hands by the interference, for the first and last
time in English history, of the head of the Catholic Church
in the relations between the Jews and the king.

At the end of 1286, Honorius IV. addressed to the
Archbishops of Canterbury[1] and York[2] and their suffragans
the following bull :—

"We have heard that in England the accursed and
perfidious Jews have done unspeakable things and horrible
acts, to the shame of our Creator and the detriment of the

---

[1] Baronius. *Annales Ecclesiastici* (ed. Theiner). XIII., 10, 11.
[2] *Révue des Études Juives*, I., 298.

Catholic faith. They are said to have a wicked and deceitful book, which they commonly call Thalmud, containing manifold abominations, falsehoods, heresies, and abuses. This damnable work they continually study, and with its nefarious contents their base thoughts are always engaged. Moreover, they set their children from their tender years to study its lethal teaching, and they do not scruple to tell them that they ought to believe in it more than in the Law of Moses. so that the said children may flee from the path of God and go astray in the devious ways of the unbelievers. Moreover, they not only attempt to entice the minds of the faithful to their pestilent sect, but also. with many gifts, they seduce to apostasy those who, led by wholesome counsel, have abjured the error of infidelity and betaken themselves to the Christian faith ; so that some, being led away by the treachery of the Jews, live with them according to their rite and law, even in the parishes in which they received new life from the sacred font of baptism : and hence arise injury to our Saviour, scandal to the faithful, and dishonour to the Christian faith. Some also who have been baptised they send to other places, in order that there they may live unknown and return to their disbelief. They invite and urgently persuade Christians to attend their synagogues on the Sabbath and on other of their solemn occasions, to hear and take part in their services, and to show reverence to the parchment-scroll or book in which their law is written, in consequence of which many Christians Judaise with the Jews.

"Moreover, they have in their households Christians whom they compel to busy themselves on Sundays and feast-days with servile tasks from which they should refrain. And so they cast opprobrium on the majesty of God. They have in their houses Christian women to bring up their children. Christian men and women dwell among them : and so it often happens, when occasion offers and the time is favourable to shameful actions, that Christian

men have unblessed intercourse with Jewish women and
Christian women with Jewish men.

" Yet Christians and Jews go on meeting in each others'
houses. They spend their leisure in banqueting and feast-
ing together, and hence the opportunity for mischief be-
comes easy. On certain days they publicly abuse Christians,
or rather curse them, and do other wicked acts which offend
God and cause the loss of souls.

" And although some of you have been often asked to
devise a fitting remedy for these things, yet you have
failed to comply. Whereat we are forced to wonder the
more, since the duty of your pastoral office binds you to
show yourselves more ready and determined than other
men to avenge the wrongs of our Saviour, and to oppose
the nefarious attempts of the foes of the Christian faith.

" An evil so dangerous must not be made light of, lest,
being neglected, it may grow great. You are bound to rise
up with ready courage against such audacity in order that it
may be completely suppressed and confounded and that the
dignity and glory of the Catholic Faith may increase. Therefore by this apostolic writing we give orders that, as the duty
of your office demands, you shall use inhibitions, spiritual
and temporal penalties, and other methods, which shall seem
good to you, and which in your preaching and at other
fitting times you shall set forth, to the end, that this dis-
ease may be checked by proper remedies. So may you
have your reward from the mercy of the Eternal King.
We shall extol in our prayers your wisdom and diligence.
Let us know fully by your letters what you do in this
matter."

X.—The Effects of the Clerical Opposition.

Edward was too religious to disregard the wishes of the
Pope, expressed thus formally and solemnly and with the
utmost strength of language. And he had special reasons
for paying heed to the words of Honorius IV., on whose
money-lenders he was dependent for loans, and whose

predecessor had, by the exercise of his spiritual powers, secured for him a tenth part of the goods of the clergy of England.[1] From the moment of the issue of the bull, the policy inaugurated by the statute of 1275 was doomed. For of the two alternatives that Edward would have had before him in any further Jewish legislation that he might have undertaken—the alternatives of the abandonment of the policy of 1275, or the extension of it by further measures for the assimilation of the status of Jews to that of Christians—the Church now demanded that he should at once adopt the former. It demanded that the Jews of England should live isolated from the Christians; and this they could do only so long as they kept to pursuits, such as usury, for the practice of which they required no connection with the organisation of a gild or a town.

For a time Edward could take no decisive measures, since when the bull reached England, he had left for Gascony.[2] In that province nothing had apparently as yet been done to satisfy the demand made by the Council of Lyons, in 1274, that alien usurers should no longer be tolerated in the land of Christians. It was hopeless to try to enforce in a distant dependency the policy that had been beset in England with so many difficulties, and had now incurred the direct opposition of the Church. The only alternative was expulsion, a measure that on French soil suggested itself the more naturally, since two French kings had practically adopted it already. Before he returned home, Edward issued an order that all Jews should leave Gascony.[3]

The application of the same measure in England was a more serious matter, since the English Jews were doubtless a much larger community than those of Gascony. But, determined not to tolerate them as usurers, and convinced

---

[1] Rymer. I., 560-1.

[2] Edward left England in May, 1286. *Florence of Worcester* (English Historical Society), II., 236.

[3] *Willelmi Rishanger Chronica et Annales* (Rolls Series), 116; *Flores Historiarum* (Rolls Series), III., 70-71.

of the hopelessness of his efforts to change them into traders, Edward had no alternative but to treat them as he had treated their coreligionists in Gascony.

No doubt he was influenced in his resolution by the members of his family and court. His wife and mother and various of his officers had been in the habit of receiving liberal grants from the property and forfeitures of the Jews.[1] They must have known that this resource was decreasing steadily, and was not worth husbanding, and they must have welcomed a measure which would bring into the King's hands a fairly large amount of spoil capable of immediate distribution. And, probably, some of the ecclesiastical members of the court felt, as his mother certainly did,[2] a religious hatred of the Jews and a religious joy at the prospect of their disappearance.

XI.—THE EXPULSION.

Of the course of events for the first few months after Edward's return to England, very meagre accounts have come down to us. His searching inquiry into the conduct of the judges during his absence[3] must have taken up most of his time and energy. As soon as he had meted out punishment to those whom he had found guilty of corruption, he turned to the Jewish question. On the 18th of July, 1290, writs were issued to the sheriffs of counties, informing them that a decree had been passed that all Jews should leave England before the feast of All Saints of that year.[4] Any who remained in the country

---

[1] *Forty-second Report of the Deputy-Keeper of the Public Records,* 593 ; *Forty-fourth Report,* 109, 295 ; *Forty-fifth Report,* 72, 163 ; *Forty-ninth Report,* 81 ; *Calendar of Patent Rolls from* 1281 *to* 1292, 62, 193 ; *Archæologia,* VI., 339 ; Madox, *History of the Exchequer,* I. 225 *w* ; 230 *b* ; 231 *l* ; John of Peckham, *Registrum Epistolarum,* II. 619 ; III., 937 ; Rogers, *Oxford City Documents* (Oxford Historical Society), 208, 219 ; Tovey, *Anglia Judaica,* 200.

[2] Gractz, *Geschichte der Juden* (Second Edition), VII., note 11.

[3] *Chronicles of Edward I. and Edward II.* (Rolls Series), I., 97 ; *The Chronicle of Pierre de Langtoft* (Rolls Series), II., 185-6.

[4] Tovey, *Anglia Judaica,* 210.

after the prescribed day were declared liable to the penalty of death.[1]

Every effort was made by the King to secure the peace and safety of the Jews during the short period for which they were allowed to remain, and in the course of their journey from their homes to the coast, and from the coast to their ultimate destination. The sheriffs were ordered to have public proclamation made that "no one within the appointed period should injure, harm, damage, or grieve them," and were to ensure, for such as chose to pay for it, a safe journey to London. The wardens of the Cinque Ports, within the district of whose jurisdiction many of the Jews would necessarily embark, received orders in the same spirit as those that had been addressed to the sheriffs of the counties. They were to see that the exiles were provided, after payment, with a safe and speedy passage across the sea, and that the poor among them were enabled to travel at cheap rates and were treated with consideration.[2] These general orders were reinforced by the issue of special writs of safe-conduct for individual Jews.[3] The exiles were allowed to carry with them all of their own property that was in their possession at the time of the issue of the decree of expulsion, together with such pledges deposited with them by Christians as were not redeemed before a fixed date. A few Jews who were high in the favour of royal personages, such as Aaron, son of Vives, who was a "chattel" of the King's brother Edmund,[4] and Cok, son of Hagin, who belonged to the Queen,[5] were allowed before their departure to sell their houses and fees to any Christian who would buy them.

On St. Denis's Day all the Jews of London started on their journey to the sea-coast.[6] The treatment that they met with was not so merciful as the king had wished.

[1] *Bartholomaei de Cotton, Historia Anglicana* (Rolls Series), p. 178.
[2] Tovey, *Anglia Judaica*, 240-2.
[3] *Ib.* 241 ; *Calendar of Patent Rolls from* 1281 *to* 1292, 378, 381, 382.
[4] *Calendar of Patent Rolls*, 379.   [5] *Ib.* 381.   [6] *Ib.* 232.

Many of the richer among them embarked with all their
property at London. At the mouth of the Thames, the
master cast anchor during the ebb-tide, so that his vessel
grounded on the sands, and invited his passengers to walk
on the shore till it was again afloat. He led them to a
great distance, so that they did not get back to the river-
side till the tide was again full. Then he ran into the
water, climbed into the ship by means of a rope, and bade
them, if they needed help, call on their Prophet Moses.
They followed him into the water, and most of them were
drowned. The sailors appropriated all that the Jews
had left on board. But subsequently the master and his
accomplices were indicted, convicted of murder, and hanged.[1]

One body of the exiles set sail for France. During their
voyage fierce storms swept the sea. Many were drowned.
Many were cast destitute on the coast that they were
seeking, and were allowed by the King to live for a time
in Amiens.[2] This act of mercy, however, called forth the
censure of the Pope, and the *Parlement de la Chandeleur*,
which met in the same year, decreed that all the Jews
from England and Gascony who had taken refuge in the
French king's dominions should leave the country by the
middle of the next Lent.[3] Another body, numbering 1,335,
and consisting, to a great extent, of the poor, went to
Flanders.[4] The only known fact that we have to guide
our conjectures as to the ultimate place of settlement of
any of those who left England is that, in a list of the inhabitants of the Paris Jewry, made four years after the
Expulsion, there appear certain names with the additions
of *l'Englische* or *l'Englais*.[5] It may well be that many Jews

[1] Walter of Hemingburgh, *Chronicon* (English Historical Society), I.,
21, 22 ; Bartholomæus Cotton, *Historia Anglicana* (Rolls Series), 178 ;
Annales Monastici, III., 362, IV., 327.

[2] *Opus Chronicorum* in *Chronicles of S. Albans, J. de Trokelowe, etc.,
Annales* (Rolls Series), 57.

[3] Lourière, *Ordonnances des Rois de la France*, I., 317.

[4] *Fortieth Report of Deputy-Keeper of Public Records*, p. 474.

[5] *Revue des Etules Juives*, Vol. I., pp. 66, 67, 69.

from England, speaking the French language, were able, in spite of the Act of the *Parlement de la Chandeleur*, to become merged in the general body of the Jews of France, who were many times as numerous as those of England had been.[1] Many, too, may have thrown in their lot with their 850,000 coreligionists of Spain.[2].

The property that the Jews left behind them in England consisted of such dwelling-houses, and other houses, as remained to them in spite of the strict conditions imposed by the Statute of 1275, of the synagogues and cemeteries of their local congregations, and of bonds partly for the repayment of money, and partly for the delivery of wool and corn for which the price had been paid in advance All fell into the hands of the King,[3] except, possibly, the houses in some of those towns, such as Hereford, Winchester, and Ipswich, of which the citizens had by the purchase of manorial rights become entitled to all fines and forfeitures.[4] The annual value of the houses, as shown in the returns made by the sheriffs, was, after allowance had been made for the right of the Capital Lords, about £130. The value of the debts, as shown in the register made by the officers of the Exchequer, was about £9,100, but the amount for realisation was diminished by the King's resolve to take from the debtors, not the full amount for which they were liable, and which, under the amended statute of the Jewry,[5] could include three years' interest, but only the bare principal that had been originally advanced. Even this was not fully collected; payment was, by the King's permission, delayed, and confirmations,

[1] Graetz, VII., 267.   [2] Ibid., 155.
[3] Langtoft, II., 189 ; Hemingburgh, II., 21 ; Madox. *Exch.*, I., 261.
[4] Johnson. *Customs of Hereford*, p. 100 ; Madox. *Firma Burgi*, 12, 19, 23. I am not at all confident of the accuracy of Mr. Johnson's statement, on which the latter half of this sentence is founded. Certainly some of the houses of the Jews of Hereford. Winchester. and Ipswich, were granted away by the king (*Lansdowne MSS.*, British Museum, Vol. 820, part 5, Transcript 4). *R t r'i Originalium* (Record Commission). I., 73b-76a.   [5] *Papers Anglo-Jewish Historical Exhibition.* p. 230.

made in 1315 and 1327, of the renunciation of interest, show how long some of the debts remained outstanding. Edward III. finally gave up the claim to all further payment.[1]

It was ordered that the houses should be sold and the proceeds devoted to pious uses.[2] But it appears that they were nearly all given away to the King's friends.[3]

XII.—THE NECESSITY FOR THE EXPULSION.

The Expulsion was not the act of a cruel king. The forbearance which marks the orders to the officers who were charged with the execution of the decree had been shown by Edward many a time before, when he protected Jews against claims too rigorously enforced, and ordered that his own rights should be waived where insistence on them would have deprived his debtors of their means of subsistence.[4]

Nor was it prompted by greed. It is true that immediately after it, and according to the account of many chroniclers, as an expression of gratitude for it, the Parliament voted a tenth and a fifteenth.[5] But this can-

---

[1] *Rotuli Parliamentorum*, I, 346b; II., 8a, 402a; *Statutes of Realm*, 1 Ed. III., Stat. 2, § 3.

[2] Tovey, 235; Prynne, *Second Demurrer*, 127; *Papers, Anglo-Jewish Historical Exhibition*, 21.

[3] A list, not quite complete, of the houses belonging to the expelled Jews is contained in the Manuscript known as *Q. R. Miscellanea* : " Jews," No. 557, 9 and 11 (Public Record Office). A list of persons who received from the King grants of Jews' houses, to hold at a nominal rental, is printed in *Rotulorum Originalium Abbreviatio* (Record Commission) pp. 73b-76b, and the deeds of gift are copied in full in *Lansdowne MSS.* (British Museum) Vol. 826, Part 5, Transcript 4. Nearly all the houses mentioned in *Q. R. Miscellanea* are granted away by deeds included in the *Rotuli Originalium* and the Lansdowne Transcript.

[4] Madox. *Exch.* I. 2, 218h, 238i, etc.; Tovey, 207; Prynne, *2nd Demurrer*, 59, 76; Rymer, *Fœdera*, 523, 598.

[5] *Chronica Monasterii de Melsa* (Rolls Series), II., 251-2. *Annales Monastici*. III., 362; W. de Hemingburgh, *Chronicon* (English Historical Society) II., 22.

not have been a bribe offered beforehand, for the writs announcing the decree were issued on the fourth day after that for which the Parliament was summoned.[1] It is impossible to suppose that in so short an interval the question was brought up, the policy chosen, the price fixed, and the decree issued. It is equally impossible that Edward's conduct should have been affected by the prospect of the confiscation of the small amount of property that the Jews left behind them.

The Expulsion was a piece of independent royal action, made necessary by the impossibility of carrying out the only alternative policy that an honourable Christian king could adopt. And the impossibility was not of Edward's making. It was the result of many causes, and the knowledge of it had been brought home to him by many proofs. The guesses of our contemporary, and all but contemporary, authorities who take on themselves to explain his action, show how many were the obstacles before which he had to confess himself vanquished. In one chronicle the Expulsion is represented as a concession to the prayer of the Pope:[2] in another, as the result of the efforts of Queen Eleanor;[3] in a third, as a measure of summary punishment against the blasphemy of the Jews, taken to give satisfaction to the English clergy:[4] in a fourth as an answer to the complaints made by the magnates of the continued prevalence of usury;[5] in a fifth as an act of conformity to public opinion;[6] in a sixth, as a reform suggested by the King's independent general enquiry into the administration of the kingdom during his absence,

---

[1] Parliament was summoned for July 15th ; see Parliamentary Paper 69, of 1878 (H. of C.) "Parliaments of England." The writs ordering the Expulsion were issued on July the 18th ; see Tovey, 240.

[2] French Chronicler of London, in Riley's *Chronicles of Old London*, 242.

[3] *Annales Monastici*, II., 409.

[4] *Ib.*, III., 361.

[5] W. de Hemingburgh, II., 20.

[6] *Chronicles of Edward I. and Edward II.* (Rolls Series) Vol. I. 99 ("Omnes Judæi .... *concedente* Rege Edwardo ..... exulantur").

and his discovery, through the complaints of the Council, of the "deceits" of the Jews.[1]

Each of these statements gives us some information as to the nature and extent of the failure of Edward's policy. None gives the true cause, for none sets before us the true position of the Jews and their relations with their neighbours. It is true that it was the bull of Honorius that finally compelled Edward to give up his attempt to assimilate the position of the Jews to that of Christian traders. It is true, no doubt, that his mother had from the first dissuaded him from generous treatment, and, perhaps, had induced him to lessen the chance of the success of his policy by asserting his right over them as over his serfs.[2] But the bull of the Pope and the personal influence of the Queen-mother were alike unnecessary. If Edward had waived all his rights, if the Church had in his reign relented towards the Jews instead of increasing its bitterness towards them, both acts of generosity would have come too late. The same causes that had made the Jews accept the position of royal usurers at the end of the eleventh century, and of royal chattels at the end of the twelfth, made it impossible for them to give up either position at the end of the thirteenth. From the moment of their arrival in England they had been hated by the common people. They never had an opportunity of acquiring interests in common with their neighbours, or of entering their social or industrial institutions. Isolation brought with it danger. For the sake of safety they had to accept royal protection ; and their protectors long held them in a close grip, until one at last refused to tolerate them under the same conditions as had satisfied his predecessors. But to

---

[1] *The Chronicle of Pierre Langtoft* (Rolls Series). II., 187-89.

[2] Cum . . concesserimus Karissimæ matri nostrae Alcanorae Reginae Angliae quod nullus Judaeus habitet vel moretur in quibuscunque villis quas ipsa mater nostra habet in dotem. . . *Papers of the Anglo-Jewish Historical Exhibition.* pp. 187-8. *Forty-fourth Report of the Deputy Keeper of the Public Records.* p. 6. Graetz, *Geschichte der Juden* (Second edition), VII., note 11.

have given them their freedom would only have been to expose them to the old dislike and the old danger. If Edward had allowed them to become citizens, and had set at naught the bull of Honorius, he would have seen the English towns refusing to support his policy and denying to the Jews the right to join the gild merchant, to learn trades and to practise them, and to enjoy the protection of municipal laws and customs.

For towards all new-comers, of whatever race or religion, the English burgesses of the Middle Ages showed a spirit of unyielding exclusiveness.[1] But the feeling against the Jews was far greater than that against any other class. Every reference to them in English literature, before the Expulsion and long after it, shows its strength and bitterness. "Hell is without light where they sing lamentations," says one poet of them.[2] Another who, writing a few years after the Expulsion, mentions the massacre at the coronation of Richard I., finds in it nothing to wonder at, and nothing to regret. To him it is only natural that "The king took it for great shame That from such unclean things as them any meat to him came."[3] The chroniclers of the time refer to them again and again, and always in the same tone of dislike. "The Jews," says Matthew Paris, in his account of one of the most cruel of Henry III.'s acts of extortion, "had nearly all their money taken from them, and yet they were not pitied, because it is proved, and is manifest, that they are continually convicted of forging charters, seals and coins."[4] "They are a sign for the nation like Cain the accursed," he says elsewhere.[5] The eulogist of Edward I., when he recounts the great deeds of his hero, tells with pride and

---

[1] Compare the treatment of the Flemings, who settled as weavers in different towns of England soon after the Conquest, but had to retreat to one district in Wales, where they lived under special royal protection. Cunningham, *The Growth of English Industry and Commerce*, 176 ; and see Gross, *Gild Merchant*, II., 155-6.

[2] Jacobs, 14.   [3] *Ibid.*, 107.

[4] *Historia Anglorum*, III., 76.   [5] *Ibid.*, III., 103.

without a word of pity how "the perfidious and un-
believing horde of Jews is driven forth from England in
one day into exile."[1] And just as no punishment that they
can suffer is regarded as too heavy for their sins, so no
story of their misdoings, whether it be of the murder of
Christian children, of insults to the Christian religion, or
of fraud on Christian debtors, is too improbable or too
brutal or too trivial to be repeated.[2]

The popular hatred showed itself in deed as well as in
word. The massacres of 1190 were imitated on a small
scale at intervals during the sojourn of the Jews in England. Bradiers and hosiers, bakers and shoemakers, tailors
and copperers, priests and Oxford scholars were all ready
to take part in the looting of a Jewry.[3]

Nor was there any influence exercised by the higher
classes to make the populace less intolerant. A great
lady declared that it was a disgrace for one of her rank to
sit in a carriage in which a Jewess had sat.[4] A great noble
thought it a good jest, when a Jew on his estate fell into a
pit on a Friday, to order that he should not be helped out
either on the Jewish Sabbath or on the Christian, in order
that the absurdity of the Mosaic legislation might be
demonstrated—at the cost, as it resulted, of the Jew's
life.[5]

Bishops supported with eagerness the charge of child-
murder repeatedly brought against the Jews,[6] though Popes
and Councils had declared it to be groundless[7]: and the
judge who showed the greatest eagerness for the punish-

[1] *Chronicles of Edward I. and Edward II.* (Rolls Series), *Commendatio Lamentabilis,* II., 14.
[2] M. Paris, *Chronica Majora,* V., 114; *Annales Monastici,* IV., 503; *Gesta Abbatum Monasterii, S. Albani* (Rolls Series), I., 471.
[3] *Annales Monastici,* IV., 91; *Norfolk Antiquarian Miscellany,* I., 331; *Forty-fourth Report of the Deputy-Keeper of the Public Records,* 188; *De Antiquis Legibus,* Camden Soc., 50; Tovey, 156; Prynne, *Second Demurrer,* 118.   [4] Jacobs, 26.
[5] W. Rishanger, *Chronica et Annales* (Rolls Series), p. 1.
[6] M. Paris, *Chronica Majora,* IV., 30, 31.
[7] Hahn, *Geschichte der Ketzer,* III., 35, n. 2.

ment of the Jewish prisoners who were accused on the
monstrous charge of having murdered Hugh of Lincoln,
was a man who was held in especial honour by his con-
temporaries as a scholar and "a circumspect and discreet
man."[1]

Thus the Christians were not likely to endure the Jews
as neighbours and fellow-workers, and the Jews, even if
they had been permitted, would have been as little willing
to live the life and follow the ordinary pursuits of citizens.
It was not that they loved usury as a calling. On the
contrary, they entered willingly into all those professions
that gave them the opportunity of being their own masters
and living according to their own fashion. Many of them
were physicians, and among the most esteemed in Europe.[2]
In Italy, where the municipal and gild organisations were
easier to enter, and less narrow and exacting in their constitution, than those of England,[3] they worked at trades.[4]
In Sicily, under Frederic II., some Jews were employed
as administrators, and many more were agriculturists.[5]
In Rome, one was treasurer of the household of Pope
Alexander III., and in Southern France another filled the
same office under Count Raymond, of Toulouse.[6]   In
Austria, they were the financial ministers of the Archduke,[7]
and in Spain, one was chamberlain to Alphonso the Wise,
and many others were in the service of the same king.[8]
In England, some Jews were attached to the Court of
Henry III., and treated with special favour ; others were
useful and valued adherents of Richard, King of the

---

[1] M. Paris, *Chronica Majora*, V. 517 ; *Annales Monastici*, I. 345.

[2] *Revue des Etudes Juives*, XVIII., 258 ; *East Anglian*, V. 10 ; Jacobs, 88-9.

[3] Perrens, *Histoire de Florence*, III., 220-1, 226, Gregorovius, *Gesch. der Stadt Rom.*, V., 308.

[4] Thomas Aquinas, *Opusculum*, XXI.

[5] Güdemann, *Gesch. des Erziehungswesens*, etc., II., 287.

[6] Güdemann, II., 71 ; *Hist. Litt. de la France*, XXVII., 520.

[7] Graetz, VII., 97.

[8] *Ib.*, 125-7.

Romans,[1] and, after the prohibition of usury, others, as we have seen, became corn-merchants, and wool-merchants.

But the whole character of the Jews, their religious beliefs, and their national hopes, were such as to make repellent to them those close relations with Christians and Englishmen which would have been necessary if they had entered into the feudal or municipal organisations of the Middle Ages. Though there was no religious obstacle to prevent them from entering a Gild, still they could not, without violating their religion, eat at a Gild feast, or take part in its religious ceremonies. Their teachers, like those of the Church, warned them against social intercourse with the Christians, " lest it might lead to inter-marriage."[2] They did not speak the English language.[3] They remained willingly outside the national and municipal life.

Their isolation caused them no sorrow. Rather must it have been dear to them as a sign that they were faithful members of the one race to which in truth they belonged, the race of Israel. The interests that filled their mind were those that were common to them, not with the inhabitants of the country in which they lived, but with their brethren in faith and race scattered throughout the world. The rapidity and copiousness with which the stream of Jewish literature poured forth in the Middle Ages, showed how unfailing was the strength of the Jewish life which was its source. In Southern Europe the Jews waged among themselves fierce controversies over problems such as were suggested by the support that some of their Rabbis gave, or appeared to give, to the Aristotelian doctrines of the eternity of matter and the uncreativeness of God.[4] Among the English Jews, and in the communities of Northern France with whom the English Jews were in continual communication, literature, though less contro-

---

[1] *Royal Letters* (Rolls Series), II., 46 ; Madox. I., 257 *g* ; Rymer, *Fœdera*, I., 356.   [2] Jacobs. 269.

[3] JEWISH QUARTERLY REVIEW, IV. 12, 551 ; *Hist. Litt. de la France*, 27, 485, 650, *sq.*

[4] *Hist. Litt. de France*, XXVII., 27. 650. *sq.*

versial and engaged with less deep questions, sufficed,
nevertheless, even better to provide continual and engros-
sing interest for the orthodox. There were read and
written, down to the last years before the Expulsion,
commentaries and super-commentaries on the Bible and
the Talmud, lexicons and grammars, treatises on ritual
and ceremonial. The Rabbis discussed what blessings it
was right to use on all the occasions of life, on rising in
the morning, or on retiring to rest at night, on eating, on
washing, on being married, on hearing thunder.[1] The
English Jews were strict observers of the ceremonial law,[2]
they made use in daily life of the minutiæ of Rabbinical
scholarship, they drew up their contracts "after the usage
of the sages,"[3] and thus, like all the Jews of mediæval
Europe, they were continually reminded, in the pursuit of
their ordinary interests and occupations, that they were a
peculiar people. How proud they were of the position is
shown by the poetical literature which, as preserved in
the Jewish prayer book, is the most precious legacy that
mediæval Judaism has left us. It was common to Jews in
all lands; it commemorated all the sorrows of their nation,
and gave expression to all their hopes. It made them
feel that, scattered as they were, they yet had a destiny
of their own, and it banished from their minds, as a
counsel of baseness, the thought of making themselves
one with the "Gentiles" around them. It reminded them
that exile and persecution, and ultimate triumph were the
appointed lot of Israel, and that the same teachers who
had prophesied that the Chosen People should suffer, had
also prophesied that in the fulness of time they should
be redeemed. They knew that in the hour of danger and
persecution there had never been wanting martyrs to
testify in death to the unity of God and to the Glory of

[1] *Hist. Litt.*, 435, 411, 462, 484, 487, 507, *sq.*; JEWISH QUARTERLY
REVIEW. IV., 25.

[2] Jacobs, 286.

[3] *Archæological Journal.* XXVIII., 180.

his Name. And they could not doubt that the Lord of
Mercy and Justice would mete out due recompense to the
oppressors and the oppressed.[1]

Thus the memory of their past, and the commonplace
occurrences of their daily life, continually strengthened
the bonds that bound Jews together after twelve centuries
of dispersion. In the thirteenth century of the Christian
era, as in the first, they still regarded the Holy Land as
their true home. Three hundred Rabbis from France and
England went thither in 1211.[2] There Jehudi Halevi
ended his days.[3] There Nachmanides taught that it was
the duty of every Jew to live, and, true to his own lesson,
he set out on his pilgrimage in the seventieth year of his age.
And in his own and the next generation many Jews from
Spain and Germany followed his example.[4] A Jewish
traveller of the Middle Ages says of certain of the communities of his coreligionists that he visited: "They are full of
hopes, and they say to one another, 'Be of good cheer,
brethren, for the salvation of the Lord will be quick as the
glancing of an eye:' and were it not that we have hitherto
doubted, and thought that the end of our Captivity has not
yet arrived, we should have been gathered together long ago.
But now this will not be till the time of song arrives, and
the sound of the turtle-dove gives warning. Then will the
message arrive, and we shall ever say 'The Name of the
Lord be exalted.'"[5]

Nowhere in Europe could such men have been content to
live the life of those around them, to bind themselves with
the ties of citizenship, to find their highest hopes on earth
in the destiny of the town, or the country, in which they
dwelt. They were but sojourners. They lived in ex-
pectation of the time when the Lord should return the
Captivity of Zion, and they should look back on their
exile as reawakened dreamers.

[1] Cf. L. Zunz, *Die Synagogale Poesie des Mittelalters*, Berlin, 1856.
[2] Graetz, VII., 6.   [3] *Ibid.*, VI.   [4] VII., 138; VII., 307-8; VII., 188-9.
[5] Benjamin of Tudela, trans. Asher, I., 163.

Without the privilege of isolation they could not live: and if in England the communities of the Gentiles had been open to them, they would never have entered them.

The Expulsion of the English Jews was an event of small importance alike in English and in Jewish history. In England the effect that it produced was barely perceptible. The loss of their capital was too slight to produce any economic change.[1] The only class that benefited from their departure was the Florentine merchants, whose trade grew from this time even greater than before.[2] Political results of importance have sometimes been attributed to the Expulsion. The victory of the towns over the King has been said to have been hastened by the loss of the financial support of the Jews.[3] But it cannot have come any the sooner for the disappearance of a community from whom the King had long ceased to get any real help in his enterprises abroad, or in his struggles at home. The trading classes still complained after the Expulsion, as they had done before it, of the prevalence of the "horrible practice of usury, which has undone many, and brought many to poverty,"[4] and the "horrible practice" prevailed none the less: and perhaps the poorer agricultural classes of England, the newly enfeoffed rent-payers, found, as did the corresponding class in France,[5] that the expulsion of the Jews only compelled them to go to more cruel moneylenders than before. The coin was clipped as regularly after the Expulsion as before it, and the Christian goldsmiths were as rigorously treated as the Jewish money-

---

[1] See the Tables in Thorold Rogers' *History of Agriculture and Prices* Vols. I. and II.

[2] Peruzzi, *Storia del Commercio e dei Banchieri de Firenze*, 175.

[3] Papers, *Anglo-Jewish Historical Exhibition*, p. 211.

[4] *Rotuli Parliamentorum*, II., 332-350.   [5] Graetz, VII., 101.

lenders had been.[1] The Church, which had helped to drive out the Jews, soon found itself in conflict with Christian heresy, compared with which Jewish unbelief was harmless.

The Jews, on their side, were driven from a land which thirty-five years earlier they had begged in vain to be allowed to leave.[2] They went forth to join the far greater bodies of their countrymen in other lands, and with them to fulfil the career of sorrow that they had begun. The loss of their inhospitable home in England was but one episode in their tragic history. From France they were again to be expelled, despoiled and destitute.[3] In Germany the blood-accusation met them as in England.[4] In Spain popular massacres and clerical persecution were already preparing the ground for the Inquisition.[5] The time was still far off when Jew and Christian could live side by side and neither suffer because he would not worship after his neighbour's fashion. That time could not come until society was more heterogeneous, and the circles of interest of ordinary men wider, than they could be in the thirteenth century, until the citizen ceased to live his life, bodily and spiritual, within the walls of his native town, under the shadow of the Church.

---

[1] J. de Trokelowe, etc., *Chronica et Annales* (Rolls Series), 58 ; Ruding *Annals of the Coinage* (Third Edition), I., 198-202.

[2] M. Paris, *Chronica Majora*, V., 441, 487.

[3] Graetz, VII., 264-7 ; Depping, 228-9.   [4] Graetz, VII., 181-8, 252.

[5] *Ibid.*, 163-4, 318-20, 363.

www.ingramcontent.com/pod-product-compliance
Lightning Source LLC
Chambersburg PA
CBHW020327090426

42735CB00009B/1430